SPIRIT-LED COMMUNITY

ALSO BY LISA ROMERO FROM STEINERBOOKS

The Inner Work Path
A Foundation for Meditative Practice
in the Light of Anthroposophy

Developing the Self
Through the Inner Work Path
in the Light of Anthroposophy

Living Inner Development
The Necessity of True Inner Development
in the Light of Anthroposophy

Sex Education and the Spirit
Understanding Our Communal Responsibility
for the Healthy Development of Gender
and Sexuality within Society

Spirit-led Community

Healing the Impact of Technology

LISA ROMERO

STEINERBOOKS | 2018

2018
SteinerBooks

An imprint of Anthroposophic Press, Inc.
610 Main Street, Great Barrington, MA 01230
www.steinerbooks.org

Copyright © 2018 by Lisa Romero. All rights reserved. No part of this book may be reproduced, stored in a retrieval system, or transmitted in any form or by any means, electronic, mechanical, photocopying, recording, or otherwise without the written permission of SteinerBooks / Anthroposophic Press, Inc.

Library of Congress Control Number: 2018930296
ISBN: 978-1-62148-215-4 (paperback)
ISBN: 978-1-62148-216-1 (eBook)

Printed in the United States of America

Contents

Introduction vii

1. Reducing the Impact of Technology on the Senses 1

2. Supporting the Living Nature of Learning 50

3. Our Individual Task toward Spirit-led Community 107

   Notes 161

*This book was written in gratitude to my
Developing the Self — Developing the World
colleagues, who dedicated their time to bringing
this work to students, parents, and teachers
in order to support community wellbeing*

Introduction

Out of the deepest insights into human development, Rudolf Steiner declared that from the twentieth century onward all human beings would be able to develop a new kind of capacity: a capacity to have knowledge of the outcome of the paths that lay before us—a capacity that would enable us to foresee the inner results of the various choices that lay before us before walking down one or another path. However, this capacity of foreseeing would need to be preceded by an essential step in human development—a step that constitutes the next stage of evolution for the human being. This step is the awakening of the higher self, which he also described as the recognition of the "second self."

In the twenty-first century, we are beginning to see this new stage of development emerging on a wider scale. Many individuals are waking up to the higher "I," to the second self. Some have taken the path of declaring this inner change to the world. Individualities like Eckhart Tolle attempt to describe this awakening of the second self. He shares what he recalls as his consciousness having the feeling, "I cannot live with myself any longer"—in other words, that a part of himself could no longer tolerate another part.[1]

Deepak Chopra describes the two selves of self-consciousness as the analyzing consciousness and the witnessing self or higher self. Others describe them in terms such as the "me-self" and the "I-AM consciousness." And still others have spoken about these two as the "everyday self" and the "true self." Even though we can see numerous individualities writing and speaking about this stage of human development, there are far more people who have taken this step within themselves than we will ever know. And many more have taken the path toward this step in such a way that, although the true self is not yet fully developed, it is still coming to expression in smaller ways or to a lesser degree.

This inner recognition of the two selves has, without doubt, partially contributed to the rise of conscious inner development and meditation practices, which are becoming necessary forms of balancing our externalized pace of life. We are seeking peace and calm within in order to combat the haste and turbulence without. Because this is a significant moment in time, in which many people are able to awaken to a new state of consciousness—a state that was once only attainable by the comparatively few—it does not take long for many individuals, participating in genuine inner practices, to become aware of this second self. The "me-self"—the everyday, workaday self—begins to be witnessed by the "observer-self," which clearly is not the same quality of consciousness as the everyday self that is bound to the sensory world.

Human consciousness, as it is today, is required to take a leap forward in development. Either it will follow the

Introduction

everyday self and unite more strongly with the material world, or it will follow the path of the higher "I" and unite freely with a spiritual life. The choice has to be made by each individual; this will eventually create a great "dividing of the ways" for humanity. The start of this divide is already happening, though not yet on the scale of what is to come. Nevertheless, within each and every human being, we are beginning to have to choose which path (or which self) we wish to "increase." This will be taking place not for a chosen few, but for the whole of humanity; this wide-scale development began at the turn of the twentieth century, and it will continue for several centuries until all individuals have freely defined their place through their actions.

Between where we are now and where we must eventually arrive lies precarious ground. Materialism is increasing at a rate that may overshadow the clarity with which we can perceive our choice. A materialism that wants to create communities of technological, artificial intelligence is already seeping into the world of the developing child, changing the very foundations upon which the free individuality is cultivated.

By wearing down the potential for the development of the free, independent individual, this circumstance serves to obscure the individual's choice as to which community to align with in the future. The foundation for the free, independent individual is laid down in childhood. The protection and care of child development must prevail if we are to postpone the effects of these forces, preventing them from creating such an obstacle before we are equipped with the necessary inner evolution that ensures our capacity for free choice.

We must be prepared, as a collective humanity, with capacities and inner strengths enabling us to freely choose the form of community life that we determine to be needed for the future of humanity. We need to establish communities that are dedicated to human freedom—communities in which the health of the community, the education of the child, and social life are imbued with impulses supportive of the cultivation of human freedom.

> You may ask which educational ideal such an attitude [that of Waldorf education] comes from; it arises from complete dedication to human freedom. And it springs from our ideal to place human beings in the world so that they can unfold individual freedom—or, at least, in such a way that physical hindrances do not prevent them from doing so.[2]

As humanity is rapidly being emancipated from engagement with the natural world, the vast majority of human beings are being raised more and more not only in a human-made world—in which the resources of the earth have been extracted and utilized for human evolution—but also in a human-invented world.

Human invention is not the same as human knowledge and human discovery. We discovered penicillin; we invented technology. How we apply these things in our community rests in our hands; and in that sense, it is dependent on our human ethics. The consequences of applying our human inventions to the world are often not apparent until years—if not generations—later. Often, even when it is not a matter of a conscious intent to do harm, harm is still being done.

A number of harmful effects have emerged through the proliferation of smartphone applications—most obviously, that of having one's capacity for attention undermined and replaced with an impulsive tendency. Research shows that most people touch or swipe their smart phones over 2,500 times per day, leaving them in a state of constant partial distraction from their actual intentions.[3]

The new technologies are flooding community life, and will continue do so. Recently, it was announced that an award of fifteen million dollars is being offered to the first company that can create a computer program capable of teaching a child to read and write within an eighteen-month time frame. Such an idea is being proclaimed as a purely benevolent advancement—an advancement that would enable us, for example, to help children in remote villages to read and write purely by means of the computer or tablet.[4] However beneficial they may appear, these developments are taking place without being informed by health-related research into the consequences of such education on child development.

Even though it is clear that harm is being inflicted upon the development of the child through the overuse of such technologies—harm that brings about changes in thinking and feeling and will impulses in a direction away from harmony and wellbeing—there nevertheless appear to be continual efforts to immerse children in this kind of technology.

> All human weaknesses will be used, especially people's vanity and lack of truthfulness, to get human beings on the wrong side.[5]

And yet, how can a community hope to stop this trend when our own thinking can be just as narrow and "outcome-based"? We have all become far more materialistic than we may have consciously chosen. We perceive these so-called advancements as inevitable and "out of our hands." We do not want our children to be left out of the technological age, even if we know that these so-called advancements are deteriorating community life. From the smallest family community to the largest collective community, negative effects are being documented.

Materialistic thinking cannot gain foreknowledge of the extraordinary consequences of making computer programs the primary educators of children. The reality is that the capacity to truly know the inner effect and outcome of these things does indeed lie within the human being's grasp; however, *this capacity itself* is being undermined by the damaging intrusions of the diverting forces of certain technologies in this materialistic age.

Technology is going to continue to develop, and we will all participate in utilizing it. We cannot stop those who are actively working in the industry toward the emergence of artificial intelligence—nor can we stop the continuing pervasiveness of the internet, which consistently nudges our will in directions we would not consciously choose. We will not stop this revolution. It is already impacting life in ways far beyond our present understanding. However, we

Introduction

can actively develop the next steps of human evolution if we wish to ensure that a spiritual ground continues to exist in earthly life—a spiritual ground that utilizes all inventions in the service of the ennoblement of the human being.

We should not see what is upon us at this time as a battle against technology, but rather as a trumpet call to wake us up and to spur us toward working intensively on a future giving rise to a community that chooses to live with spiritual impulses—and, to work just as intensively as do those who strive toward a future community dominated by corporations that utilize artificial intelligence to realize what they envision. We progress not by drawing the battle lines against technology and its "internet of things," but rather by being a fighter for the spirit.

Through my experience of working directly with numerous people on the theme of inner development over the course of many years, it has become clear to me that a new awakening is readily available to all who work toward it. The capacities are being developed, and through them more and more people are making clear choices for supporting a community led by the spirit.

However, it is also clear that some people are greatly hindered by the imbalances that were impressed upon them during their development as a child. This can divert the awakening of the next steps of their potential adult development. It is becoming clearer that through the direction we are heading in as a culture, this phenomenon is growing worse because the restless mechanical world is affecting what we find when we turn toward our inner life.

> Restlessness and nervousness are the first fruits of a materialistic civilization.... It has already become an exceptional achievement if anyone succeeds in maintaining a state of inner peace and concentration. But only by wresting inward peace from the turmoil and pace of our civilization, and through achieving a union with the powers of a higher world, can we preserve our humanity.[6]

The understanding that by the end of this age, humanity is going to be divided into two distinct communities is not only spoken of by individuals like Rudolf Steiner, but it is also given, in one form or another, in all the great cosmologies. Although these pictures are often misread by organized religions—who tend to understand them in the sense of one religion prevailing over the other or one religion being "of God," but not the other—the picture of the "dividing of the ways" has nevertheless always been present. Only individuals of the present age can read them with the understanding relevant to our time.

In the future, one community will have grown together with machines while following the path of materialistic invention; it will have corporations as its leadership. The other community will have developed the next inner capacities required for our ongoing evolution as human beings. Those community members will have awakened these new capacities within their consciousness by their own efforts. And, consequently, they will have formed a new community life led by spiritual motivations.

Introduction

Many individuals—even half of the world's population—will at some point, from now onward, out of the nature of the times, begin to take this progressive path in human development, developing from out of themselves the higher consciousness that already lives within them in seed form. By the end of this age, it will be clear that, through their actions, all individuals have placed themselves in one community or the other.

From out of this development of the second self—the higher self—the next capacity is developed. Along with other attributes, this capacity will allow us to foresee the outcomes of the choices that lay before us. Through the awakening of the higher self, we will be able to cultivate this foreseeing capacity. Then each person will know what part of the human being is "increased" by engaging with one thing or another. Each will be free to choose which aspects of themselves will increase and which ones will decrease.

Each individual must themselves undertake this necessary stage of development; *we alone* must chose how we will walk into the future. For those individuals who choose the path of higher development, this path will lead them to develop a direct, living connection with spiritual insight. It will then be possible for those individuals, in freedom, to come together with others who also bear these developed capacities. They may then choose to build new community forms that do not harm, but that create, support, and ennoble humanity.

These new community forms will serve to develop community from out of the spiritual insights and impulses gained through these new capacities. This means that spiritual impulses will play a part in all that we do in terms of developing community in the world.

> Nothing but the will to conduct life spiritually—the will to allow spiritual decisions, spiritual impulses, to play a part in what we do in the physical world—can make humanity healthy again.[7]

Those who do not work consciously to take this step of developing the higher consciousness within themselves may consciously choose to bind themselves with all that is external and transitory in human life, and in this way grow together with artificial intelligence, uniting their own consciousness with that of machines. This is already beginning to happen, but without individuals really being aware of it. Our time, energy, and attention are being diverted.

The inner health that enables the individual human being to choose the path of human progress leading to the health of the community is being placed under greater and greater threat by the impulses arising from materialism. These impulses already impact the development of the child by creating imbalances in the inner life, which eventually disturb their capacity for free, self-determined choices as adults. The adult makes decisions regarding where to place their time, energy, and attention in the unfolding of their individual life. This is their contribution to community life and therefore to the development of humanity as a whole.

By understanding the importance of health in childhood and its repercussions in adulthood, we can give the individual the best possible chance of establishing within themselves the freedom to choose which path they will take as the future of humanity progresses. As adults, we must awake to the salutary path for humanity before those possessing the materialistic view of the world take further steps. Otherwise, we will continue on this path of world destruction through the limitations of those who are leading the world into the future through their current positions of power.

My work is primarily within the field of adult education through inner development and meditation. It is therefore only from a particular point of view that I will try to offer a small contribution to the understanding of the importance of the task that lies ahead of all of us.

Many other people may have other points of view and far greater experience in the realm of child development. It is the parents, teachers, and community members who have a direct influence on what surrounds the developing child, and who can implement the healthy forms of education that our future community needs.

What is given in this book in relationship to child development has arisen not only out of my years of experience working as a health practitioner in the light of Anthroposophy, but also out of a dedication to the anthroposophic path of inner development, which awakens faculties beyond what can be worked out by the intellect.

I owe all these insights to the workings of the spirituality in which we may participate because of the evolutionary path laid out before humanity, if we choose to take it. Therefore, this is not a "do's and don'ts" book about how to raise a child. It is primarily intended to support the inner development path for adults and to reinforce an understanding for the importance of our collective task. In the light gained from the inner work path, this book will explore the foundations of child development that serve as a basis for the inner development of adults. And the individual adult's free choice to walk upon this inner path is essential for the next stages of our collective world development.

> We must understand that strength and energy, perseverance and a holy enthusiasm, are necessary to transform into spirituality the intellectualism that, after all, belongs to the present age. These things are necessary so that the thoughts and ideas of human beings today may rise into the spiritual world and that the human being may find the path of ideas upward to the spirit no less than downward into nature. And if we would understand this, then we must fully realize that intellectualism, to begin with, offers the greatest imaginable hindrance to the revelation of any spiritual content that is present within the soul.[8]

Through conscious inner development and spiritual grace, courageous people will lead the world's development to unfold toward the light that shines in the good, the harmonious, and the true for the generations to come.

I

Reducing the Impact of Technology on the Senses

The human being is born into the physical world, and from the earliest stages of growth in the womb they begin their education and development under the influences of the earthly world and its inhabitants. As the child is born, the community they are born into continuously educates them; whether in their smaller family community or in the wider community, they are continuously learning through how they are treated and related to, and through the surrounding environment. This is an education not only through the kingdoms of nature but also through the human-made environment, both of which are introduced to the growing child according to the understanding, values, and resources of the community.

This complex education provided by the outer world develops the child's inner world: their thinking, their feeling, and their impulses of will. Being born into a small village community of hunters and gatherers would create for us an "inner-world education" vastly different from what would result by being born into a more human-made environment and a community able to provide complex resources.

Even before birth, we are shaped, formed, and impacted by the environment surrounding us. Everything within the environment that can be perceived by the senses—through the impressions and stimuli of the sensory world—impacts the developing child. All that enters us from the outside—such as food, air, water, temperature, light, and so on, as well as the effects of relationships and events in our life—not only becomes our experience, but it also becomes our body and our inner world.

Natural environments and the kingdoms of nature play a lesser role in the process of raising a child today than they did even one hundred years ago. And in our time, each generation is increasingly being educated more through the "invented" world than through the natural world. This has consequences on child development. A child who is raised on the invented technology of the internet has a different inner development in their thinking, feeling, and the impulses for their will from a child raised primarily on an engagement with the wisdom of nature, its resources, and the creativity of the transformed natural world.

Technology that is designed to form unhealthy habits of thinking, feeling, and will impulses in the child in order to increase monetary wealth for others is immoral technology, immoral education.

We have entered the era where intentional immorality is raising the next generation. An unethical inventor is being given just as much opportunity to influence the young as an ethical scientist like Albert Einstein, who stands humbly in his task.

> My religiosity consists in a humble admiration of the infinitely superior spirit that reveals itself in the little that we, with our weak and transitory understanding, can comprehend of reality. (Albert Einstein)[9]

The inner education of the next generation takes place within the life of the community, whether we like it or not, whether it is healthy or not, and whether it is true or not (what is healthy and what is true could be seen as the same thing).

The collective consciousness of the community inscribes itself upon the child, as does the outer environment. Rudolf Steiner stated that each community has its own consciousness body, and that by age six we are already deeply conditioned by the collective consciousness of the community we are born into. This conditioning continues throughout our school life, and therefore it can be heavily influenced by our formal education.

The attitudes and beliefs of individuals are many and varied, but it is the collective consciousness—with its collective dominance—that produces the effects that influence the individual child to the greatest degree. It is not an individual's belief, but the combined belief of the community that has the greater power in terms of determining what the community comes to regard as healthy and necessary resources. These resources are then implemented into the community in all its forms, from health care and education to the structure of buildings, etc. Our whole outer environment is created by the community intentions from the past, and this is the basic foundation of the child's education.

The collective consciousness includes the values, beliefs, virtues, vices, laws, and attributes of not only the few family members around us, but of the whole community with which we engage. This "inscription" of the collective consciousness upon us can be narrow or diverse, harmonious or disharmonious. It can develop in us a sense for the good, the harmonious, and the true; or it can give rise to unethical forms of community life through its conditioning.

The inscription of the collective consciousness upon us, throughout childhood, has also conditioned our thinking, our feeling, and our will impulses. All human capacities that are conditioned in this way are not free in terms of their *content*; they are free only in their *capacity*. The capacity for thought belongs to the spirit-willed nature of the human being. The content of our thinking is for the most part dependent upon our environment and our education. The capacity for thinking aligns us with the freedom we so desire; the content, on the other hand, is inscribed by the outer world's current stage of development.

As adults, when we consider our inner world, we usually believe this inner world to be ours alone. More than anywhere else, it is here that we imagine our individual freedom to be. It is where we believe that we can think what we want to think, feel what we want to feel, and do what we want to do. Much of human ingenuity has had the aim of cultivating ways of increasing this so-called individual freedom. We generally believe that the more resources we have, the more choices we have, and that therefore the more individual freedom we have.

However, in terms of the content, the vast majority of our thinking, feeling, and willing is not free because it is not even our own. We think thoughts that we have been educated to think, we feel certain ways about things because of the way we have been educated to feel about them. Most of the time, our thinking is a reaction to the environment around us—an environment provided to us by the thoughts of others, which have become outer reality in the form of our shared community life. Our common thinking is our community education.

As this community education is taking place, the child is also developing their first milestone in the "education of self-awareness," which is the awaking realization of the duality of self and other.

The first educational phase of the individuality of the child is undergone through being born into the duality of the physical, sense-perceptible world. None of the forms of education entailed in this would be possible without the senses and the nervous system. It is through the senses that the child awakens and takes in the educational experiences of the world outside of them, while simultaneously awakening to the sense of self. Without the senses and nervous system, we would be unable to participate in our further education by means of the community and the larger world. We would also be unable to participate in our further education in terms of gaining knowledge about ourselves. A feeling for "what is self" and "what is other" is cultivated through the development and care of the senses and the nervous system.

We can glean the importance for our development of the healthy senses by looking into both the outer world and ourselves. Through understanding the workings of this dual reality, we can perceive how the senses are the gateway for the entirety of our earthly education.

Try some basic exercises (these exercises are not for children, but only for adults). Beginning with the sense of touch, take in your hands a piece of clothing that you're wearing, move your fingers to explore the material, and focus all your attention on the quality of the cloth. Try to purely engage your attention—and not your intellect—to arrive at an assessment of the quality of the cloth; allow yourself to sense and experience what this other "thing" is like.

Without changing what you are doing with your hands, without changing the way you are touching or moving the cloth, place your attention on your skin that is touching the cloth. Place your attention on your sense of touch rather than what you are touching.

You can now go back to the awareness of touching the cloth, of what the cloth itself feels like. And once you feel yourself absorbed in "the other"—which in this case is the cloth—then return again to focusing attention on your hand and the sense of touch that is doing the touching.

What do we recognize through this simple exercise? We recognize that when our attention is placed on the cloth we are touching and its qualities, then these qualities of the cloth, of the other, become clearer to us than they are when our attention is placed on our own skin and sense of touching. We can also perceive that when we focus on our sense of touch through our skin, we experience a stronger sense of self. And when we focus on the cloth, we have a stronger sense of the other. We can see in the sense of touch what the German poet Novalis stated: that the sense of touch is both a uniting and a separating. On one hand, I can unite myself with the other in order to know the other thing. Simultaneously, I recognize that I am a being separate from this other thing.

The sense of touch clearly shows us that the senses awaken our consciousness to both the reality of the other, the world, and the reality of ourselves.

Let us try another exercise with the senses: this time with the sense of smell. Smell the back of your hand; what is this smell like? Put all your attention on trying to smell what is there, on trying to discern the quality.

Then turn your attention to the sense of smell itself—not to the nature of the thing you smell, but to the smelling itself.

Once again, we experience a heightened perception of the smell of the other when we focus on what we smell, and we experience a stronger sense of self when we focus on the smeller or the sense of smell itself.

For the incarnating spirit, the senses are the doorway to an awareness of the duality of the physical world.

Return to the touch exercise, this time focusing not only on the sense of "the other" (the material) and its quality or on the sense of self that is touching, but also try to awaken to the recognition of the freely directed *will* that moves your attention between self and other. This recognition is the first seed of our becoming aware of the individualized free will, which appears not as content but as an activity brought about in the present moment. The individual free will is the living, present will capacity.

Through the world of the senses, we can perceive where the seed of our freedom expresses itself.

All that is truly free first begins in the form of an active *capacity*, not in the form of *content*. It is this free activity that is of the spirit. The content, however, may not be free, even if it expresses our so-called personal preferences. It is here that the idea of individuality awakens in a new light: *individuality as the free, liberated part of the human being*—not as the particular likes and dislikes of the individual appearing as a personality.

All that is free is of the spirit. The higher "I" is the name given to that individualized spirit spark.

The free, individualized will is the third attribute of the previous exercise involving awakening to duality through the senses. It makes up the trinity of the experience: self, other, and individualized will. The third aspect of this trinity, the unseen spirit, is brought to realization from out of the reality of the sense-perceptible duality of self and other.

The spirit is revealed between the duality of self and other. Yet it appears as neither self nor other. If it is self, then it is also other.

From this perspective, the mystery of our life—the qualitative nature of our "separated self," together with our individual destiny—is the working of the higher "I." Through seeing life in this way, we may come to understand the mystic words of the Sufi poet Rumi: "What you seek is also seeking you."[10]

The senses simultaneously bring to us our experiences of the world and of our separated self. We are being educated into the world of duality. But yes, this world of duality is where the principle that overcomes the duality—the spirit as the individualized expression of the higher "I"—can first be awakened.

Generally, for most individuals, this awakening does not come in the form of a great, momentous revelation; it usually does not take two years to integrate the experience, as it did with Eckhart Tolle, for example. For most individuals, the first seed of the recognition of the higher "I" is experiencing the awareness of the individualized free will—the free will by means of which we can direct our attention to self or to other. We can summarize the nature of this individualized free will as: That in me which directs my attention between the "sense of self" and the "sense of other." This is not "will" in the sense that we say one has a "strong or weak will," as this belongs to the everyday self; rather, this is the free will that is individual to each person.

When we use the free will within our inner capacity for attention, this activates the "witnessing self."

This "sense of self" that we experience through our sensory system, and through our separation from the sensory world around us, is not the higher "I," but the ground of the "me-self"—the separated, everyday self. Of course, the momentary perception of the second self—the higher "I" that can be experienced as the individualized free will directing these activities of the senses—is not the full reality of the awakened higher "I" experience, but only a glimpse of something in me that lies beyond the personal, everyday self. The everyday self is the principle upon which our world and our communities have, for the most part, been founded. Rudolf Steiner was emphasizing that we all have the capacity to grow beyond this when he stated that teachers should hang their everyday, workaday self outside the classroom before they enter. He obviously felt that they have something else available to them, inwardly, with which to enter the classroom.

This all seems simple enough, perhaps too simple. However, it is nevertheless true: the care and development of the senses in childhood is the essential ground for fluid progress in the adult's path of inner development. If the three aspects of the trinity, demonstrated through the above exercises, are clear for you, then it is quite likely that there is a form of wholeness in your own sensory system. Either this has occurred through the care and development of the senses in childhood, or by the independent development of your individualized will as an adult, which would have required a special effort on your part—or both.

This higher "I" awakening belongs to the present evolutionary path, which continues the progress and development of the individual and of humanity. What Rudolf Steiner presented as the "twentieth-century clairvoyance" has been available since the turn of the twentieth century to the many, and not just to a chosen few. It is cultivated in esoteric schooling by individuals who, consciously, through the effort of their individualized will, apply themselves to certain inner exercises or contemplations. (Many of these exercises are presented, along with a guiding form for their application, in my first book: *The Inner Work Path*.[11]) The first form of education in the conscious schooling path is an education toward becoming conscious of the presence of the spiritual world. This is achieved through an inner path of development leading to an awakening of the presence of the "second self" or higher "I."

The second self could not be developed with such relative ease, and in full consciousness, if the foundational "sense of self" and "sense of other" were not healthily formed.

Rudolf Steiner expressed this healthy sense of self as the *eternal masculine* force in every human being; and he expressed the capacity to experience the other, to devote ourselves to the other, as the *eternal feminine* force in every human being. Reverence for what lies beyond the sensory world is born from the development of both forces together: the healthy sense of self and devotion to the other.

Even if the senses are well cared for, the influence of intellectualism early on in the growing child's world can carve away at the natural sense of wonder that lives in the child's nature. This sense of wonder can be schooled into veneration and reverence through the adults surrounding the child.

The child has to be introduced into the world of the senses, into the world of duality, in a healthy way, so that they can awaken the next step of human development out of themselves in freedom. What will happen if the individuals within humanity do not awaken to the higher self, to the next step in human development? We have reached a time when the strongest of consequences will arise if we do not take the next step in the development of our human capacities: to awaken the spiritual self and develop capacities that create community led by spiritual motivations.

So much more of our essential inner life than we are generally aware of depends upon a healthy development of the senses. All inner experiences founded on the duality of self and other require the healthy functioning of senses for their cultivation. For example, in order to have *respect*, there has to be a healthy relationship between self and other. Another capacity resulting from the healthy development of the sensory system is our capacity for *veneration*. These capacities are needed in child development, most notably because all that is laid down in childhood is renewed on the path of inner development. Veneration is also central to the path of inner development. However, here we are no longer concerned with the veneration of persons as we often are in childhood, but rather with the veneration of truth and higher knowledge.

> It must be emphasized that higher cognition is not concerned with the veneration of persons, but the veneration of truth and knowledge.... In an epoch of criticism, ideals are lowered; other feelings take the place of veneration, respect, adoration, and wonder. Our own

age thrusts these feelings further and further into the background.... Veneration, homage, devotion, are like nutriment making the soul healthy and strong—especially strong for the activity of cognition. Disrespect, antipathy, underestimation of what deserves recognition, all exert a paralyzing and withering effect on this faculty of cognition.[12]

A healthy sense of self and the capacity to devote ourselves to the experience of the other is the basis on which the individual can stand in healthy relationship to the sensory world. It is also the necessary ground for the development of our conscious relationship to the spiritual world. Through the relationship of the eternal masculine and the eternal feminine within the individual, the higher "I" can be awakened.

For every human being bears within themselves a higher self, besides what we may call the workaday self. This higher self remains hidden until it is awakened. And each human being can themselves alone awaken this higher being within themselves. As long as this higher being is not awakened, the higher faculties slumbering in every human being, and leading to suprasensory knowledge, will remain concealed.[13]

The spiritual world lies concealed from the workaday, everyday self—just as it does from the current, sense-perceptible worldview resounding in the collective consciousness, which is the initial source of conditioning for the everyday self.

I Would Be Glad

You are sitting in a wagon being
drawn by a horse
whose reins
you hold.

There are two inside of you
who can steer.

Though most never hand the reins to Me
so they go from place to place the
best they can, though
rarely happy.

And rarely does their whole body laugh
feeling God's poke
in the
ribs.

If you ever feel tired, dear,
my shoulder is soft,
I'd be glad to
steer a
while.

—*Kabir*[14]

For those involved in the training of inner development and meditation, the individualized free will is consistently being applied to certain exercises and formulas in the form of a daily practice. This results in the growth and development of the consciousness of the second self. This is a marked step on the path of inner development—an essential step, which brings about the recognition that the spirit does indeed exist, because the awakened spirit within one now confirms it! At this point, it is a definite reality, and no matter how much this reality is denied by the materialistic science of the time, it cannot be denied in the one who has had this direct experience.

Through the continual inner practice of meditation and contemplation—along with encountering the inner resistance to engaging with these inner practices and the inevitable trials that arise through taking hold of ourselves—the individual becomes aware that these two selves have their orientations in different directions, as the German poet Goethe describes in his *Faust*:

> In me there are two souls, alas, and their
> Division tears my life in two.
> One loves the world, it clutches her, it binds
> Itself to her, clinging with furious lust;
> The other longs to soar beyond the dust
> Into the realm of high ancestral minds.[15]

The reason the awakening of the higher "I" is the most significant step on the path of inner development is that the will activity of the higher "I" must be engaged in the act of self-transformation. If we do not first engage the will activity of the higher "I," then genuine self-transformation cannot truly take place. Instead, in its place, we would experience the split between my ideas about "how I would like to see myself" (the "preferred particular self" or everyday self) and the reality of all the parts of ourselves that we wish to overcome (the not-so-admired particular, everyday self).

Utilizing the unfree, personal self in the exercises—no matter how strong our personal will is—inevitably leads to the personal growth of the everyday self. We could say that our personal, individual growth (in the sense of the separated self) continues on its way, but now with the additional guise of inner development as a new persona for the everyday self. This can lead us even further from the genuine path that is intended to lead humanity forward.

> All knowledge pursued merely for the enrichment of personal learning and the accumulation of personal treasure leads you away from the path; but all knowledge pursued for growth to ripeness within the process of human ennoblement and cosmic development brings you a step forward.[16]

If, however, the higher self has awakened, and if out of its free will activity (all of its activity is free) we take hold of the reins of our own self, then genuine transformation may take place. It is in the course of this genuine transformation that the higher self emerges to greater and greater degrees. The spark eventually lights the wick and we perceive the flame. The flame of the candle continues to shine through the transformation of the candle wax into light. This willingness to transform what is "me-self," the candle wax, into the higher "I," the light or flame, consistently engages the free activity of the higher self.

Once we understand the importance of the individual's process of awakening through the duality of the self and the other—which is facilitated through our sensory experience—we can recognize the value of the duality that our sensory-based consciousness brings us. Things perceived in life without the senses, without this duality of self and other, could not reveal the spirit. The care and development of the senses in early childhood supports our ability, acquired through this duality, to clearly find the spiritual principle that is beyond the dual nature of life. This spiritual principle in us awakens the reality of the spiritual principle in the other.

> In ordinary, everyday life, we do not wake up in the encounter with what is going on in the depths of the soul or spirit of another person; we wake up in the encounter with their natural aspects.... Just as a person wakes up through the natural world surrounding him in the right way in everyday life, sensing light and tone—so do we wake up rightly, at a higher level, in the encounter with the soul–spirit of our fellow human beings.[17]

Development and Care of the Senses

We are typically aware of the five senses, but Rudolf Steiner, among others, describes not only the five obvious senses, but also suggests that when these senses are investigated and refined we can begin to understand that there are actually twelve senses through which we awaken to the world and ourselves. These twelve senses work together to make a whole, and it is through the combining of these senses—which awaken before birth—that the young child, through the care and development of the senses, grows the capacities required to develop independent learning. To be able to become an independent learner, the child must have the capacities of *attention, self-regulation,* and *healthy attachment.* These three components, necessary for learning in all educational systems and within life itself, are the consequence of the care and development the twelve senses in the first seven years of life.

If a school child is unable to engage the capacities of attention, self-regulation, and attachment, then they are unable to participate in the conscious learning process. We could say that nearly all the diagnoses given to children today in the sense of learning difficulties are the result of not having the three foundations of learning; or, we could say that nearly all learning difficulties arise from a combination of one or more imbalances in these three foundations.

The twelve senses, working as a whole, develop these three foundations. If certain senses are greatly overstimulated, such as the senses of sight and hearing, then as adults we may need to gravitate to the opposite in order to form a balance. It is no wonder, then, that methods such as yoga have been taken up in a strong way in the Western cities alongside the rise of technologically stimulated lives.

The other senses, such as the senses of balance and movement, which are greatly underdeveloped in modern life, give us, as adults, the recognition that we need to spend our so-called recreation time remedying the imbalance. Even if we don't actually get a chance to remedy these aspects, we can feel that they are missing.

For children, the consequences are greater—firstly, because they are still developing; and secondly, because without the wholeness of the senses they cannot come to the state of school readiness, which begins with *learning how to learn* and in turn becomes a capacity for full, independent learning.

The twelve senses are as follows:

> Sense of touch (basic pressure and texture sense)
> Sense of life (covers wellbeing)
> Sense of movement (covers both vibration and motility)
> Sense of balance and weight
> Sense of smell
> Sense of taste
> Sense of sight
> Sense of warmth or temperature
> Sense of hearing
> Sense of word
> Sense of thought
> Sense of "I"

If certain senses are greatly overstimulated—such as the senses of sight and hearing—and other senses are greatly underdeveloped—such as the senses of balance and movement, as has become the case with the rise of technology in the young child's life—then we see a deficit in the three primary learning capacities. If certain senses are adulterated—such as the senses of taste and smell, as they have become with a junk food diet—then this, too, can affect the healthy care and development for the child's sensory and nervous system.

It is, however, also useful to recognize that each child has a predisposition, from their individual constitution, to have what might be termed a "hyper" or "hypo" tendency in each of the senses. This is quite different from an overstimulation or an underactivity, or the adulteration of the senses inflicted on them by the world into which they are born.

The tendency of the child for a hyper or hypo experience helps those around the child to enter into relationship with this child as an individual. We have to learn, with them, how the world affects them. They demand not merely a generic type of parenting, but a parenting tailored to their individual needs. We come to know what is in them as their nature, and we are able, through the right kind of nurturing, to get to know the expressions of this individual being in relationship to the world and to ourselves. In the age of individuality, this understanding does not come instinctively; rather, it must be newly awakened within us if we are to find the right relationship to each other, and even to our own children.

> As this era progresses, people will find it more and more difficult to relate to each other correctly, because bringing ourselves into relationships correctly requires inner development, inner activity.[18]

By understanding and clarifying the hyper and hypo sense tendencies, we come to realize that we cannot treat every child in the same manner. We have to individualize our approach to each child's care and development. The extraordinary relationship that the primary caregiver brings to this individual child serves to support the wholeness of that child's relationship to self and other for the rest of their life.

Many people affected by disturbances to their sensory development are unable to find themselves in the right relationship to the world. They feel that they have no place in the community or that they don't fit into society.

This is not out of a strengthened confidence of the fullness of their individuality and who they choose to be, but out of a discord between self and other. The primary caregiver in the first seven years of life serves the most important role in terms of helping the child to establish the foundations they need in order to connect with community throughout the rest of their life. The younger the child, the more intensively important it is for the caregiver to cultivate the senses in the right way. This is due to the importance of the "lower senses" for facilitating the growth of the "upper senses" in the later years (for more on this, see the *EduCareDo* lessons).[19] The right care and development of the senses is the most important role for laying the foundations in all human-to-human development.

Hyper and hypo senses help us understand the individual child and the effects of daily life upon them. What is right for one child may not be right for another; what one child needs as conscious attention to certain senses may not be necessary for another. Through this understanding, we can help to bring a balance to the senses in an individual way. In the first seven years of life, the most possible holistic care and development of all twelve senses is the best ground we can give to the child.

The senses and the nervous system continue to develop into adulthood—especially the upper senses—but the foundations of all twelve in the first seven years of life need to be held as healthily as possible. Below are some examples of identifying and understanding the individual's experience; in each individual, each sense may be different. Therefore, exploring the way these individualized senses combine to give a person a unique way of sensing the world and themselves, is a part of our process of connecting with the young child. But examples will also be given into adulthood, so that we may also see these various differences in ourselves.

All children "on the spectrum" have more intensive responses to their own hyper and hypo senses, and by this means they indicate to us how we need to treat each child individually. Our capacity for perceiving these indications is becoming a necessity, as all of those who are on the spectrum demand it of us. There is no possibility of a healthy "conveyer-belt upbringing" in our age, and as we progress forward this will increasingly be the case. The "spectrum" children are waking us up to this fact at a rapid rate. They insist that we not lag behind in developing an individualized approach to care and understanding for every child, even if they do not outwardly demand it of us.

Adults who are living in an imbalanced way because of modern lifestyles can also evaluate how their own senses are either under-supported or overstimulated by the demands of life. Through self-evaluation, we can correct them consciously ourselves. However, this is relatively easy to do only if the senses have been reasonably cared for in term of their foundational development during the first seven years of life.

Adults who have had a strong disturbance of their senses in childhood will need to correct that disturbance through their own awakened spiritual will. This is possible through vigorous and committed inner work. Thus, through developing the "I," the disturbed sensory system will no longer disturb.

Below is a small introduction to understanding and supporting the senses. Further in-depth understanding of this complex system, as well as examples of how they come to expression in others—including useful natural remedies (compresses, footbaths, and so on) that serve to harmonize the senses—are provided on the website *DevelopingTheSelf.org*, on the page: "The Care and Development of the Senses."

Sense of Touch

Hyper sense of touch:

Babies demand to be held, swaddled, and positioned in a particular way in order to be settled because they experience all the variances in pressure from what or who is touching them. These babies can seem fussier than normal, or highly strung. The child can be disturbed by sensations against their skin; particular clothing fibers or textures can be irritating and may hurt them. Even being tickled can be experienced as painful. From the outside, they might seem jumpy when they are approached. They tend to be fussy about who touches them, often preferring only the primary caregivers to carry and hold them because they are most closely acquainted with them. If they are cuddly, they will want cuddles only on their terms and are choosy about the people with whom they are tactile.

The older child might complain about being threatened by others and push them away; or they may remove themselves and spend a lot of time avoiding others. They can tend toward creating and maintaining inflexible physical boundaries. Despite this, they may let others take advantage of them when the touch is pleasurable because they can lose themselves in it. The type of touch they want can be very specific, and they may not return the affection. Hyper touch can also include the preference or dislike of certain textures of food. As an adult, in order to trust a partner, they may show a need to feel safe by having control over the way they are touched.

Hypo sense of touch:

Babies settle best when they have something touching most of their body surface. They may push against swaddling, but this resistance helps them to settle. These babies can seem more settled; they can be happy in a variety of sleep positions and places. The child extends and pushes their body until they feel the boundary. For some children, this includes bumping into things and others, doorways, etc. Occasionally this can manifest to the point of repeatedly hitting their head or body against hard surfaces. They are very tactile and will tend to touch most things they see with varying amounts of pressure. In order to be satisfied, they may need to touch a lot or be touched a lot. Older children may still rely upon external pressure against their skin to maintain a sense of self, thriving on contact sports or friendships that allow physical contact.

Bedding and clothing illustrate how we can make a difference to the pressure experienced through the sense of touch. Swaddling a baby with a hyper sense of touch gives them the security they need in order to settle, and the quality of the pressure and of the fabric is important. They may need a light wool wrap that has a little stretch, so that they feel the firmness for security but are not overpowered by the pressure. A baby with a hypo sense of touch is also made to feel secure by swaddling, but they may need a thicker, firmer fabric, and may need to be regularly rewrapped, sometimes with varying fabrics.

The same principle applies to older children. Woolen blankets provide more weight and protection than lighter quilts, whereas soft sheets made of cotton, silk, or linen can be varied according to the sensitivity of the child. This also occurs with clothing: the child with a hyper sense of touch will need a particular weight and texture, while the child with a hypo sense of touch will settle best with weight upon them. For example, wearing a weightier piece of clothing on their upper body can often help calm a child with a hypo sense of touch at school. One of the best things we can do to support the sense of touch in children is to give firm but warm and loving physical boundaries. This can help the child with a hyper sense of touch to feel safe, to extend their exploration without becoming "lost" or frightened, and it can help the child with a hypo sense of touch to meet themselves within the boundary provided.

Support:

In both hyper and hypo, we can create opportunities for experiencing the polarities, for example: light silks and heavy stones, rough barks and slippery shells, spiky ferns and spongy petals, soft pillows and hard benches. Between the polarities, the consciousness of differentiation arises. It creates an inner flexibility. An inner movement is awakened through touching living fibers, and the person has to bring something of themselves to meet the outer object. This is the health-giving effect of natural objects in relation to the sense of touch.

A hyper sense of touch can also be addressed by developing an appreciation and sensitivity for all things. A hypo sense of touch can benefit from regular, familiar experiences that develop sensitivity and differentiation. There are a number of useful activities involving organic, natural objects, through which a person can practice "pushing against" and "shaping out of their own activity," thereby helping them to develop a healthy sense of touch—for example, gardening, lifting rocks and digging, modeling clay, carving, sculpting, and woodwork.

Balancing the senses, including the sense of touch:

Create a harmonious, balanced experience. The rose's archetypal quality of harmony and balance, for example—which comes to expression in the plant's threefold blossom, leaf, and root system—is an all-encompassing beneficial substance for those with either a hyper or hypo sense of touch. Lavender and rosemary address other particular tendencies in the senses: that is, lavender nourishes and calms the nerves, and rosemary has a warming and enlivening effect, particularly on the metabolism. Each of the last two plants directs a particular function; whereas the rose harmonizes all the functions (see *DevelopingTheSelf.org*).

Sense of Life

Hyper sense of life:

The baby may constantly cry from seemingly small discomforts or changes. The slightest wind in the bowels can keep them awake. They have a low pain threshold and are very fussy. They are overwhelmed by the slightest disturbance to the system: a dirty diaper, a small cut, a change in routine, a new food. The child will take time to assimilate the new. They are consumed by the pain of the experience and feel as if everything else has to be stopped until order is returned. It can be difficult for the caregiver to find what will help them settle. If the aggravating factor is ignored or even given too much attention, the child can feel overcome, overwhelmed. An older child or adult may avoid certain foods or experiences, as they perceive variations in the way things affect them, and may make them feel unwell; or they may avoid these things simply because they don't like to change something within themselves to meet the unfamiliar.

Hypo sense of life:

Having a hypo sense of life may lead to a lack of awareness of the fact that there is disorder in the body and that something needs to be done to bring about harmony. The baby will not complain of a dirty diaper and will seem to be easygoing. The child can appear to be able to skip meals and not need healthy rhythms, but this can show as irritability, which they may not connect to the hunger and lack of nourishment. It can take a lot to hurt or bother the child. At bedtime, they might say they are not tired, but will fall asleep easily. They can be injured or sick, but not realize it or complain. Adults with a hypo sense of life may lack rhythm and routine and push themselves to the limit, often being able to ignore signs of sickness. Bringing attention to the contrast between a sense of wellbeing and the discord of overextending themselves can help them to recognize these behaviors.

Support:

The hypersensitive child requires more experiences of being able to bring forward their own healing capacities in order to make things right again: to experience disorder, then re-order. When they hurt themselves, it can be helpful to reduce other sensory stimulation and to give them plenty of time to recover, acknowledging the discomfort and letting them know they are doing a good job and that "I can see you're starting to get better." They may need to complain by crying while transitioning to sleep, or through the discomfort.

Reducing the Impact of Technology on the Senses

For a child with a hypo sense of life, the injury needs to be treated, even though they may not think so. They need to have their attention drawn to it with Band-Aids, bandages, and so on, especially since it is easily forgotten and may become infected without their being aware of it. They have to learn to pay attention to changes in their body. Put an emphasis on the transition time between activities so they learn to recognize the inner shift that happens when one thing ends and another starts, for example: stopping to take shoes off at the door, and lining them up neatly before going inside.

SENSE OF MOVEMENT

Hyper sense of movement:

This is when a child has an over-awareness of where their body is in space, which causes tension and over-focusing. They are poised and ready to catch the ball, but they reach for it too soon and miss it. They make false starts in races. Too much movement can be disorienting and scary, so they tend not to take risks. They try really hard to get things right, going over and over the same movement with gritted teeth and tension, for example: in writing, the letter is over-inscribed onto the page. The shape is very fixed. They have an image of what is coming and they control their body to meet it, but it can be hard to let the image unfold naturally into the whole form. An over-anticipation. When they enter a new space, they can be cautious about where they position themselves. They may stutter and try to correct the forms they are creating with their speech. They could complain that the other children are moving about too much, so that they can't get their work done, and possibly even feel sick when looking at things moving outside of themselves. The movement of the car puts them to, and any external movement that overrides their own movement easily hypnotizes them.

Hypo sense of movement:

Here the child has a lack of awareness of both their own movement and their absence of movement. They may move a lot but are not really aware of what they are doing, or if anything is in their way. Other times, they may lie about and not respond to instructions. They are fearless but also accident prone, as their lack of spatial orientation makes it hard to get their attention. Skipping is difficult, as well as judging when to make a move; crossing the road can be dangerous. They act before they think. The same goes for moving their limbs; they put themselves into all sorts of positions because it stimulates their sense of movement. They deny hitting others, even though it was their limb that did it.

Support:

It helps to have a lot of physical–motor activities that have a purpose and a rhythm, including: gardening, climbing, walking, building, and preparing for seasonal changes. Moving from inside play to outside play, from tiny cubbies to expansive fields, experiencing how the position and movement of the body has to change in different environments. Moving things into position, lining them up, and making patterns—for example, with rocks or wooden blocks. Folding cloths and sheets with another person: having to meet each other's fingers to catch the corner of the cloth, and then walking backward to open the cloth out again—and repeating the steps, coming closer each time. Games such as "Simon says," "musical chairs," and "statues." Songs with rhythm and body gestures: Hearing beautifully formed sounds and words and copying them. Learning more than one language in order to expand the shape and movement of the mouth and broaden the child's relationship to words. Tongue twisters and books full of rhymes that encourage the eyes and the mouth to keep up with, and catch on to, the patterns. Making the eyes focus on distance and then on close vision, on moving and then on still objects. Reduce the amount of technology and screen time, as it has a deleterious effect on the sense of movement. A home-nursing application of a chamomile compress over the abdomen helps to calm the nervous system and brings warmth for movement into the metabolism and limbs. This is particularly helpful for hypersensitive people. Skin brushing can help hyposensitive people.

Sense of Balance

Hyper sense of balance:

There is the tendency to not take risks for fear of falling. The child feels wobbly as soon as they put one foot onto the balance beam, so they pull back. They easily feel disorientated. When they physically spin around, it takes them a long time to stop the inner spinning.

Hypo sense of balance:

Here the child often has difficulty maintaining balance while climbing or walking on uneven surfaces. They fall frequently, though they can continue to engage in risky activities because of a poor capacity to gauge the equilibrium required. When sitting, the tendency is to lean to one side. It is difficult for them to stay upright against gravity, so they lean on doorways, furniture, and so on.

Support:

Encourage being able to return to uprightness against gravity, for example: jumping from heights and standing up, using stilts and bicycles, crossing wobbly bridges, and walking on rocks around a garden's edge. Balance can be harmonized through playing "statues," knitting, weaving, ball sports, and games where the midline has to be crossed on the vertical and horizontal planes. Having to make things balance, such as constructing towers with a variety of organically shaped objects, as well as building projects and sculpting with clay, sand, and wax.

Also useful are "form drawing," and moving in patterns such as a figure eight. Pushing wheelbarrows of dirt, digging holes, and filling pots with dirt use the sense of balance to hold the weight and perceive the right measure. Provide ergonomic furniture that encourages effort in uprightness, without overusing this furniture. A home-nursing application of a quark compress over the chest and a footbath that alternates between bowls of hot and cold water awakens the middle space, the point of balance. Lemon footbaths can also be grounding, which helps establish a starting place for the inner sense of balance.

Sense of Smell

Hyper sense of smell:

The child may be disturbed by aromas, even their own. The smell of someone else can be overpowering and make them move away. The smell of someone or something can prevent them from wanting to know more about that person or thing—or they could become infatuated, unable to let go of that person or thing. They can distinguish between variations in aroma, and some variations can make them feel unwell. If the food is "off," they will be the first to say so.

Hypo sense of smell:

The child may recognize their own smell, and can become quite attached to it. They can have quite a strong body odor and yet it may not affect them. But they often find it more difficult to identify other aromas. They will put something right up to their nose and have a good deep sniff. They may eat or drink things that are "off" and not notice; and they mingle with others easily, not being put off by much.

Support:

We can educate the child to recognize that a smell teaches us something, and that we may like or dislike the smell—but that we can also have wonder for what makes it that way, in order to be able to understand it. Encourage them to trust their sense of smell as a way of helping to discover the truth. Keep cleaning scents and other unnecessary aromas to a minimum. Add natural aromas and oils for medicinal purposes and bring natural seasonal scents into the home only to balance the space, not for unnecessary reasons. Play games with blindfolds in order to practice identifying different smells.

Sense of Taste

Hyper sense of taste:

Here the child can often taste every little difference; they can be very discerning. They choose bland food and eat a limited variety, going for familiar textures and flavors, often separating foods rather than mixing them up. They could be overcome by the taste of something they don't like and withdraw from eating it, but they could also want to eat a lot of another food because they lose themselves in the experience of enjoying it. Other people can "leave a bad taste in their mouth." The child may stop eating in order to reduce the impact of other senses, because food is something that they can control and prevent from entering them. Their sense of fashion and social skills can be immature.

Hypo sense of taste:

Here there is often a lack of discernment in terms of what they put in their mouth; needing strong substances in order to be satisfied. If they don't know their own taste, they can follow fads in fashion, food, and lifestyle; they can be overcome by the influence of society and peers. They don't mind trying something, especially if it brings about a sensation that they like, or helps them to fit in.

Support:

Make eating a joy and a social occasion. Help the hypersensitive child to relate through something else that they are familiar with, such as shaping things with their hands. It can also help to have different parts or components of the meal on separate individual serving plates, with the rule that everyone can eat as much as they like but they have to have a little bit of everything. This can also help those with a hypo sense of taste to come to know each food on its own and refine their discernment. It can also be a joy to wonder what is in the stew and learn to discern the individual ingredients within a combined arrangement. Offer food that is full of life at a similar time each day, because the functions of the organs are best prepared by keeping to the same rhythm. Vitality occurs as a result of our ability to denature a substance different from what already lives in us; and this can indirectly improve our social skills, because here, too, we have to mix ourselves with something other than ourselves and bear it. Speak about food with wonder for its qualities, beauty, and the way it grows in the world. Make the surroundings beautiful and tasteful.

Sense of Sight

Hyper sense of sight:

Here light can cause discomfort; it can be piercing and intolerable, perhaps causing pain and ill health in other parts of the body. The child generally doesn't tolerate light well and has less of a need for it.

Hypo sense of sight:

They are generally long- or shortsighted, tending toward blindness because more light is needed. This causes a lack of differentiation in forms and makes some things blurry. They might prefer to have the light on, though if they stay with what is familiar, they will prefer the dark.

Support:

Retain joy and wonder in each task so that more of the world can reveal itself. The world should be a colorful and exciting place for us as young adults when we have been nourished with a social life that is warm, tasteful, and true. Apply this to architecture, furnishings, wall colors, clothing, and activities. The application of chamomile over the abdomen can help to calm the nervous system and alleviate pain from overexposure to light.

Sense of Warmth

Hyper sense of warmth:

Oversensitive to changes in the outside temperature, the child can be overcome by heat or cold. They will carry lots of clothes in order to be able to make themselves comfortable, or they may avoid places because they won't be able to cope with the temperature.

Hypo sense of warmth:

Here there is often a lack of awareness of one's own bodily temperature in relation to the environment. Sometimes they feel hot on the surface, but their internal organs are not warm enough. They may under-dress or over-dress, unable to determine the appropriate clothing for the environment. They will stay in the water or rain until their lips are blue and they have goose bumps, all the time denying the experience that they are cold. Likewise, they are prone to being overexposed to heat.

Support:

It is greatly supportive to have a warm home and warm relationships; showing interest in your children is very important for the sense of warmth. Very small children always need an extra layer of clothing. Have a house rule that incorporates wearing socks and/or house shoes and having the body dressed warmly, including covering the chest, kidney region, calves, and feet. Natural fibers let the body breathe, and wool insulates and regulates temperature much better than cotton. Cotton is suitable for warm environments. Allow the adolescent to have more of a say in what they wear when they go out; and if the sense of warmth has been adequately developed, they will have a healthy gauge of how many layers to wear. Use real-life seasonal changes as indications to awaken the adolescent's own relationship to their inner authority about what to wear, so that it becomes a conversation that they have with the world as opposed to a matter of parental authority.

Combating the elements—whether rain, hail, or shine—while dressed in adequate attire can strengthen the sense of warmth. Try not to make the inside temperature very cold when the outside temperature is very warm, so that the difference is not extreme. Until children are about five years old, the caregiver needs to remove and add the layers. Until they are about fourteen years old, caregivers need to remind them to take the layers on and off and teach them healthy durations for exposure to extreme temperatures. Treat the body with protective body oil and the application of heat. Nutritional baths, which leave a layer of protein on the skin and generate warmth from the inside, can be used as long as no prescribed or recreational drugs are being taken. Lemon footbaths draw the warmth to the feet and distribute it throughout the body. Use hot water bottles in bed. Directions for all of these applications are given in more detail at *DevelopingTheSelf.org*.

Sense of Hearing

Hyper sense of hearing:

The child is often oversensitive to sound to the point of pain if it is out of key, tone, pitch, or rhythm, or if it is too loud or too soft. Their inner space feels penetrated and they may leave the room or area, or put their hands over their ears in order to block the sound. They have an ability to discern individual sounds and they enter deeply into the sound, losing themselves in it; or they can be disturbed by the sound and not want to enter into it. They feel the resonance that is left in the space.

Hypo sense of hearing:

They often lack the ability to differentiate various sounds, tending toward deafness. They can't assess the pitch, and they may not notice the resonance or differentiation that the tone has left in the space. They don't have a relationship to their inner space as an individual standing separate from others. They may not realize whether they are using a loud or a quiet voice, and also may not necessarily change it to suit the environment.

Support:

The sense of hearing can be developed through listening to live music, through which we can truly meet the other behind the sound. Encourage the desire to enter into a seeking for the inner balance or source of the tone, and of the resonance that remains in the space. Sing a variety of songs, rhythms, and harmonies around the home. The pentatonic scale can only produce harmony, and therefore it can be used to harmonize the sense of hearing. Provide handmade instruments and natural objects in order to practice listening to the different sounds that can be created. Let the adolescent experiment with a wide variety of musical styles, sounds, and noises, but also give them something by which to gauge their taste, and the volume, so that they can come toward a healthy measure and a wide variety of music.

Sense of Word

Hyper sense of word:

The child can become caught up in what is going on outside of them, and may interrupt communication. They can be fixated on the words used, thereby missing the meaning that one is trying to convey. They fall into the other's words, and into the art or the drama that they are watching.

Hypo sense of word:

They can't connect to other's words, the piece of art they are looking at, or even the signpost. They don't understand the meaning that is conveyed. There is a slow response and slow process of recognition; they have to gather the word by repeating what has been said or looking at the piece of art over and over again.

Support:

Everything that harmonizes and develops vocabulary supports the sense of word. Adults can also study history, as well as the way symbols are used in myths, legends, and languages. Speech exercises and stimulating conversations keep the mind flexible. It helps to use a wide variety of words around the developing child: choosing different words to express the same thing, as well as playing with words, can help to expand the sense of word.

Sense of Thought

Hyper sense of thought:

The child may feel as though everyone thinks differently from them, and they can also become engrossed in the other's thoughts to the point that they lose their own thoughts. They can agree with the concepts that the other is expressing, but they lose themselves in the "equation" and can be easily convinced to completely change their opinion or point of view. They can perceive patterns and systems, but can become caught in them as if they are a maze, sometimes losing the connection to the rest of their life.

Hypo sense of thought:

There can be difficulty in merging with and following the other's train of thought. Instead of being able to perceive the other's thoughts, they can only perceive the same thing they were already thinking, and may not be able to discern that it is different than the other person's thought.

They often find themselves in unclear agreements, because they mistakenly thought the other person agreed with them. They relate what they hear to their own thoughts instead of recognizing differences—as though they don't realize there are differing points of view.

Support:

Harmonizing the sense of life also harmonizes the sense of thought. Children can be read traditional Grimm's fairy tales and share in prayers and verses, which serve to build a reverent relationship to something greater than the material self. These practices are also beneficial for adults, as is poetry, history, art exhibitions, and forms of spiritual development that strengthen the individual's relationship to the truth, to the harmony of the cosmos, and to the meaning of life.

Sense of "I"

Hyper sense of "I":

When alone, the child can have a strong connection to their own point of view—but when mingling with others, they may find it difficult to have or maintain their own experience. They may drop their own point of view and take on that of another. Others can influence their decisions and actions and easily overpower them. They may lose themselves to another, falling in love easily. They can wake up if another enters their room at night—or they may not be able to sleep if a familiar other is not present.

Reducing the Impact of Technology on the Senses

They find it difficult to focus on themselves when someone else is in the home, even if they are in another room.

Hypo sense of "I":

They can have difficulty falling deeply in love, but instead have many shallow relationships. They can cross the boundaries on a physical and emotional level, as they don't experience that the other is their own person—that the other has their own inner life and that they experience the world in an individual, unique way. They can overlook the fact that others are walking in and out of their space, acting as if these others were not there. They can concentrate in a crowd just as easily as by themselves. They can disregard the individuality of the other, treating them solely according to outer characteristics such as "male or female," or "young or old."

Support:

It helps to develop and uphold household rules that are not based on one person's preferences, but that take into account all members of the family and their needs. Treat others according to their individuality and do not discriminate against them because of outer characteristics or traits.

Through our relationship to the vast sensory world, we experience the various senses. However, we do so in the context of an increasingly limited exposure to this vast world. As technology proliferates and the presence of the natural world in our lives diminishes, our healthy foundations are threatened—even to the point where we may no longer be able to register the imbalance. Through developing a conscious relationship to the care and development of the senses, we can begin to reestablish the ability to know how to maintain a healthy balance. Through consciously caring for the senses in childhood, the right foundations are laid. The senses establish the right relationship to the world for our continued growth and development. The higher senses are still developing, and they will play a greater role in the future of humanity than they do today.

In the sensory world, with our individualized body—by which we are separated from the world around us—whatever we want to see in the physical world can only be seen from a particular point of view. Literally, we each have a different point of view according to where and how we stand and look out into the world. The hyper and hypo senses further color that point of view. We all have a place from which to begin exploring the world. It is important, even though we may never understand why, that we help each child to come into themselves—to attain their vantage point for viewing the world—in order that they can grow confidently into the world and eventually, from there, grow beyond the sensory world.

For the spiritual researcher, this is a reality that is proven through the spiritual inquiry toward truth. In such an inquiry, we find that, in a certain way, the point of view "opposite" our own is actually the other half of the truth that we have yet to discover. In fact, Rudolf Steiner said that in true inquiry we can attempt to look at something from twelve points of view.

Therefore, as a spiritual researcher, oppositional ideas are an understandable fact. When we hear another's point of view, we feel no need to defend our own point of view or diminish the person who brings a different one, but rather we try to gain insight—through our fellow travelers—of the facets that we have not directly explored ourselves. This helps us to expand our capacity to see further and from various points of view. It gives us an opportunity to not only humble ourselves, but to open ourselves to the unfolding mystery that only reveals itself to us in portions.

> Every one who is seriously involved in the pursuit of science becomes convinced that a spirit is manifest in the laws of the Universe—a spirit vastly superior to that of man, and one in the face of which we with our modest powers must feel humble. In this way the pursuit of science leads to a religious feeling of a special sort, which is indeed quite different from the religiosity of someone more naïve. (Albert Einstein)[20]

Through the physical body and the twelve senses, we stand as a separate individual in the sensory world with only one point of view: the one in which we are standing. In the spiritual world, I may eventually awaken to all twelve points of view simultaneously, even though the soul may be able to experience the sensory world from only one point of view at a time. However, it is useful to have the ability to find our way via spiritual insight, so that we are not taken off track by what seem to be explorations opposite to the one, single truth. Instead, spiritual insight enables us to return back to a point of reference. Therefore, our earthly task becomes our "point of view" in our spiritual inquiry (this is explored further in chapter 3).

It would be difficult to speak clearly while embracing two opposite points of view in a single expression, but this embrace of two opposing points of view can be experienced as a reality by the "I" in the spiritual world. This is expressed in the Eastern traditions as the snake devouring its own tail.

In this way, although we may express into our outer world that which we discover as spiritual realities in our own unique way—through the way we live into the world around us—we will not find ourselves shut up in our own point of view, but rather open to the points of view of others. This brings us into a growing harmony with the whole sphere of life.

Saint John of the Cross and Saint Teresa of Avila are known to have been friends, and yet in reading their poetry we can at times read expressions of their individual points of view regarding certain spiritual realities that seem to oppose one another. And yet we do not feel conflicted, but rather rounded out by their apparent discrepancies; they expand our perception rather than creating a division for us.

The Servant of Unity

Most men in power have not the strength or wisdom
    to be satisfied with the way things are.
The sane know contentment, for beauty is their lover,
    and beauty is never absent from this world.

Reducing the Impact of Technology on the Senses

The farther away light is from one's touch
   the more one naturally speaks of the
   need for change.
Yes, overthrow any government inside
   that makes you weep.
The child complains about the external and focuses his
   energies there;
   the warrior conquers the realms within
   and becomes gifted.
Only the inspired should make decisions
   that affect the lives of many,
Never a man who has not held God in his arms
   and become the servant of unity.
   —*St. Teresa of Avila*[21]

Now, a different point of view; this was not from an enemy, but a community member, colleague, and friend.

They Have Different Needs

Some of the seeds beneath the earth
   are dormant.
They fell the last time the cool air
   turned the leaves gold.
Those seeds have different needs than we do;
   let them go about their life
   completely unharmed
   by your views.
We have cracked open, we sensed
   even beneath the earth—
   the holy was near,
and are reaching up to know
   and claim light
   as our self. —*St. John of the Cross*[22]

Having another point of view does not weaken us, but strengthens us; spiritual diversity is how we understand the many facets of the spirit. Above, in the first poem, we are shown how only the truly inspired views should lead the world in a way that affects the lives of others—while in the second poem, we are directed to not disturb those with different points of view, letting them go about their lives unaffected by our own view. Both perspectives are true and have their own strengthening effects.

If this is the case—that other spiritual points of view strengthen us—then why is it that there are so many difficulties between people who are walking a spiritual path? This problem faces many groups of people who are working collectively to form a relationship to spiritual insight; there emerge difficult social problems between members of such groups. One reason is that spiritual insight pursued merely for the acquisition of greater personal knowledge, or to confirm previously formed personal beliefs, distorts the insight itself. Spiritual knowledge pursued to improve ourselves and our ability to give to others has different results.

> Someone who forms his conceptions of the higher world with pretensions carried over from life on the physical plane can say to an associate who has a different view of things, "You are a stupid fellow," or a bad man, or the like.... If one knows the reasons why an unbrotherly spirit can so easily crop up in just those societies built on a spiritual foundation, one also knows how such a danger can be avoided by undertaking to transform one's soul orientation when one joins with others in cultivating knowledge of the higher worlds.[23]

Visiting Holy Shrines

> If you circumambulated every holy shrine in the world
> ten times,
> it would not get you to heaven
> as quick
> as controlling your
> anger. —*Kabir*[24]

If we are to transform community from the materialistic path that is set on dividing us according to outer rules, then not only must we first set about transforming ourselves—but then, we must set about joining with others who also want to take on this transformation within themselves. By working with these others, we can strengthen the impulses of the spirit not only in ourselves, but into the community.

Whichever way we are strengthened—whether through our direct, awakened connection to the spiritual world, or through joining with the striving of our colleagues and friends who also know for themselves the need for such awakening—we can unite in creating new community forms. Working from the spirit toward community life is a task that cannot be achieved alone. The very nature of the task requires groups of individuals to bring about true change on the level of community. However, it does not require as many people as we might think; as few as seven individuals can begin working to create a new community led by the spirit.

2

Supporting the Living Nature of Learning

Life processes allow the outer world to penetrate deeper into our inner world, shaping and forming it. Through the gateway of the senses, the outer world can be taken in and transformed into our inner world. We do this both with the food we take in for the body, and with the "food" we take in for the soul. To be a citizen of this world, we have to take nourishment into ourselves and transform it. We would not survive long without engaging in this process of taking in food, transforming it within us, and thereby sustaining ourselves.

Our "digesting of the world" is an extraordinary thing; we can all take in the same food, and yet, out of that same physical substance, we create our individualized protein, our individualized physical body. We can also produce energy, which each of us is able to utilize through our individual will, potentially in a completely unique way.

The taking in of the world, the digesting of it, and the building up of our own being from it, relies on the activity of the life processes. Although they are the most essential processes for sustaining our being, we are for the most part unaware of them because they lie below the threshold of human consciousness.

The seven life processes are designated as follows:

> Breathing
> Warming
> Nourishing
> Secreting
> Maintaining
> Growing
> Reproducing

Breathing is the name of the first life process. It is where we begin—between the outer world and the inner world. When we eat some food, we must take it in; the senses stand together with the first life process at the threshold of the inner world, because they allow us to perceive the outer thing. The first life process is named *breathing* because this "taking in" occurs—just like breathing—in a rhythmic way. Although our eyes are consistently open while we are engaging our sense of sight, through the life process we "breathe in" perceptions in a rhythmic way.

We do not eat nonstop; we eat and then take a break from eating. All of the senses work in this rhythmic way, even though we are not always conscious of it. This occurs because of the first life process.

After taking in the food substance via the guardian of the senses, we now need to chew the food. We begin to change it from the state that it was in while outside of us; we begin adapting it, in our mouth, to our inner world.

This life process is called *warming*—the process of adapting what is outer to the inner conditions of our digestion.

Our next step is to completely overcome the food's own nature; we have to denature the food. It is by means of this overcoming of the nature of the food that we dissolve it into its essential building blocks; this is the life process called *nourishing*. It is an apt name, as it has been seen that simply giving human beings the end results of digestion alone—the vitamins, minerals, amino acids, etc.—will not suffice to nourish us. Even though we know the exact chemical components needed to sustain the body, something more takes place in the Krebs cycle—the cellular metabolism—that is not yet fully understood. Astronauts have proven that we require real food for nourishment, not just pills. The nourishment we gain from denaturing the food ourselves is more than just the end product. It is the *process of denaturing the food*—so that the "otherness" is overcome—that produces healthy effects; this process is connected with the life process of *nourishing*.

The next stage of digestive activity is to sort out what parts of the food substance we need to keep and allow into the inner systems of the body, and which need to be secreted or eliminated as unnecessary. This step is connected to the life process of *secreting*. Secreting provides us with the building blocks (from the carbohydrates, proteins, fats, and so on) that we individually require, and eliminates what we do not need. We can now utilize these building blocks by maintaining and replenishing our body

Supporting the Living Nature of Learning

and sustaining our energy; the life process of *maintaining* is most active here.

Maintaining and replenishing is not all that is needed; we also require forces for the *growth* and repair of our bodily structures, not only to replenish and maintain what we have. All parts of the body require growth or regeneration to varying degrees, even once the body has reached its mature, adult proportions. Constant transformation and renewal take place; these processes also give us the energy to transform the world through our deeds, to act in new ways, and to create the new. The final life process—that of *reproducing*—creates new cells and new growth.

We take in this physical world, and through the life processes—through digestion—the outer world is transformed; it either becomes more of my body or it becomes energy through which I can continue to act in the outside world.

As food comes into our body, we must determine if it is good for us to eat. If it is spoiled food, then it must be eliminated. There are three thresholds it has to pass. The mouth is the first threshold. We can spit it out of the mouth because it does not taste right, or we can decide not to put it into our mouth because it does not smell right. The senses let us know if this food is okay for us, if it is of good quality; if the food is fresh or old, or has begun to decay.

If the food passes this threshold of the senses, it can still be eliminated and prevented from crossing the second threshold of the stomach. We can vomit up the food, we can prevent it from going further inside us. However, if it does pass from the stomach into the intestines, before it crosses the boundary of the intestinal wall we can evacuate it through the third threshold, diarrhea, which is a way of guarding the body by quickly eliminating the substance from the bowel so that little is absorbed through the intestinal wall. Once it has passed through the intestinal wall, it is now truly inside us, and only immune–defense responses can attempt to rid us of an unwanted foreign substance.

The senses are the gateway between the outer world and the inner world. Through our life processes we transform what was once outside us—what was once "other"—into what is now inside and what we call "self."

Through the unconscious life processes—through the transformation of the outer substances of the world—the outer physical substance now becomes my inner physical substance. These same life processes not only help to build the bodily "me," but they also help to create the other aspects of me. Building up my body and building up my "me-self" both occur as a result of taking from the outer world, the "other," into the inner world of self. All the impressions and sensations, all the thoughts and feelings of the outer world become my inner world, thus feeding the "me-self." The everyday self also grows up through the life processes.

It is essential that the child grows and learns from this world in order to become a citizen of the earthly world in the fullest sense. The child does this naturally through the life processes; from the very beginnings of life, the child is already learning through the life processes. Unconsciously, the outer world is becoming the inner world through the natural, unconscious functions of the life processes.

What would be left of me if everything that could be built up and sustained in me from the external world were taken away? The body cannot be sustained without taking the outer world into my inner world in order to create and maintain itself. My sense of self could not be sustained in this world without taking the outer world into my inner world, thereby creating and maintaining the everyday "me."

The everyday self, the "me-self" that has to participate in this world, is built up through the outer world becoming the inner world. It is developed, conditioned, and educated through the capacity—engendered by means of the life processes—to unite self with other, to take the "outer world" across the thresholds of the self and become as one with it.

Children are naturally open to this process of "outer becoming inner"; the younger the person, the more dynamic this openness is.

Formal education of the child goes beyond the education acquired through living life and through experiencing the surrounding community. However, the child's community and surrounding environment are their foundational educators.

Formal education is what we choose to teach the child; this includes what we as a community believe that they need to know. As you can well imagine, education in one part of the world could look entirely different from education in another part of the world.

Even within the same country, cultures educate differently. In many cases, we are educating children according to certain preferences: namely, that a certain community's beliefs need to be passed on to the child. This can be seen explicitly in history education. The history given to the children of indigenous cultures by their own elders would naturally be entirely different than the history given to the children of the modern people occupying that country. History is, for the most part, written and determined so that it best serves the community teaching it. The formal education, given by whatever group of people to its own children, is generally concerned with conveying a particular content.

Content can be good, harmonious, and true—or it can be preferred information, persuasive information, convenient information, according to who wants to shape the future of the community and into what orientation of inner content they want to direct the everyday self's beliefs.

The *way* the content is delivered also changes its capacity to nourish the individual soul—or to leave it malnourished. Intellectual content, prescriptive content, and the mere presentation of information nourishes the inner world differently than does content that engages the capacity to think and feel. When we engage the capacities of thinking and feeling, this is a very different experience than just passing on the information that seeks to "fill" the thinking with its own abstract content.

Let's try an exercise in order to follow how what is outside us affects our inner world in different ways.

Read the following two pieces of content aloud; this method will produce a clearer experience for most people. And hearing someone else read these two pieces aloud can make the experience even clearer.

While doing this, observe the nature of your own inner experience, and keep reading the recipe, or the passage from Rudolf Steiner, until you feel you have a grasp of what each is activating in you. You may wish to try each several times. Try to observe the quality of your thinking and feeling as these thoughts that you engage with impress themselves upon you.

Recipe for layered chocolate tart

The ingredients for the filling are as follows:

> 435g (3 cups) cashews
> 75g (1/2 cup) hazelnuts, roasted and skinned
> 60ml (1/4 cup) warm water
> 2 tablespoons raw cacao powder
> 125ml (1/2 cup) maple syrup
> 75g dark chocolate (85% cocoa), melted
> 1/4 teaspoon sea salt
> 350ml coconut milk
> 175ml melted coconut oil
> 2 teaspoons vanilla extract
> 80ml (1/3 cup) freshly brewed espresso
> Roasted hazelnuts, extra, chopped, to serve
> Raw cacao nibs

The ingredients for the base are listed below:

> 80g (1/2 cup) cashews, roasted
> 45g (1/4 cup) hazelnuts, roasted and skinned

55g (1/4 cup) raw buckwheat, roasted
35g (1/3 cup) dried coconut, toasted
1 tablespoon raw cacao powder
160g fresh Medjool dates, pitted and chopped
1 tablespoon coconut oil
A pinch of sea salt

Method

Place 2 cups cashews in a bowl. Place remaining cashews in a separate bowl. Fill both bowls with cold water. Set aside for 4–6 hours to soak. Rinse under cold running water and drain, keeping separate.

Release base of a 20 cm. (base measurement) springform pan. Invert. Spray with oil. Line with baking paper, allowing a 4 cm. overhang. Secure in the pan. Grease and line side of pan with baking paper, extending 1 cm. above rim.

For the base, process roasted cashews, hazelnuts, buckwheat, coconut, and cacao until finely chopped. Add dates, oil, and salt. Process until well combined and sticky. Press into base of prepared pan. Use a straight-sided glass to smooth the surface. Place in freezer for 30 minutes or until firm.

Use a high-speed blender to blend the hazelnuts, water, cacao, and 100 ml. maple syrup, scraping down the sides occasionally, until smooth. Add chocolate and salt. Blend until smooth. Add 2 cups soaked cashews, 270 ml. coconut milk, 125 ml. coconut oil, and 1 teaspoon vanilla. Blend until very smooth. Transfer to a bowl. Clean the blender.

For the coffee layer, use the blender to blend the espresso and remaining soaked cashews, 80 ml. coconut milk, 50 ml. coconut oil, 25 ml. maple syrup, and vanilla, scraping down the sides occasionally, until very smooth. Transfer to a separate bowl.

> Pour one-third of the chocolate mixture into the prepared pan. Gently tap on the side of the pan to smooth the surface. Place in the freezer for one hour or until firm. Pour half the coffee mixture into the prepared pan. Gently tap on the side of the pan to smooth the surface. Repeat, in three more layers, with remaining chocolate mixture and coffee mixture, freezing for one hour between layers and finishing with chocolate mixture. Place in the freezer for eight hours or overnight to set.
>
> Before serving, transfer cake to the fridge for 1 hour to soften slightly.

If you feel you have been able to follow this "recipe thinking" inwardly, then try to perceive the differences produced by following the next text from a lecture by Rudolf Steiner on heart thinking.[25]

> In giving descriptions from the spiritual worlds, in translating our experiences into terms of logical thought, we feel as if we were approaching a hill on which there are wonderful rock formations that must be hewn out to build houses for human beings. In the same way, our experiences in the spiritual worlds have to be translated into logical thoughts. When anyone wants to communicate to other human beings what they have experienced through the thinking of the heart, they, too, must translate it into logical thoughts. But logical thoughts are merely the language in which, in spiritual science, the thinking of the heart is communicated. There may be someone who finds difficulty in the communications of a genuine spiritual investigator, and says, "I hear only words; they convey no thoughts to me." That may be the fault of the one who is speaking, but not necessarily so; it may be the fault of the listener who can hear only the sound of the words and is incapable of advancing from the words

to the thoughts. It may be the fault of a person who clothes allegedly spiritual truths in thoughts that fail to convey to others any evidence of the thinking of the heart. But it may equally be the fault of the listener who is incapable of detecting these truths behind the thoughts, which are like words conveying the findings of the thinking of the heart.

Whatever can be communicated to humankind from the thinking of the heart must be capable of being cast into clearly formulated thoughts. If this is not possible, then it is not ready to be communicated. The touchstone is whether the experiences can be translated into lucid words and clearly defined thoughts. Thus, even when we hear the deepest truths of the heart stated in words, we must accustom ourselves to perceiving behind them the thought forms and their content. The student of spiritual science must acquire this faculty if they wish to help in spreading through humankind whatever can be revealed from the spirit. It would be sheer egoism if anyone wished to have it for themselves alone; mystical experiences, like intellectual experiences, must become the common heritage of humankind. Only by realizing this can we understand the mission of spiritual science for humankind—a mission that must become increasingly effective as time goes on.

We can recognize that the thoughts of the recipe and the thoughts achieved through spiritual science produce different inner effects. They should do so, unless our own life processes are no longer flexible. Many adults, by the time they are in their thirties, begin to lose the flexibility of the life processes. For some, this takes place at a much earlier age.

By the time we reach adulthood, the outer world has filled up our inner world. We have a strong sense of self. And we often wish to maintain that self rather than continue to grow. Being full of ourselves, we begin to use the life processes just to validate the "me-self." We stop learning and, in a way, become hardened egos. This process occurs at some point for every human being today unless they consciously work against the sclerotic ageing process of the materialistically imbued inner world to re-enliven themselves.

Through our digestive activity, we renew ourselves every seven years. But in our "me-self," some people harden in ways that close them off from the outer world, to the point that they are almost entirely unable to continue learning and evolving. If we would spend as much time on "inner youth" as we tend to on outer youth, we would not fall into the hands of the hardening forces.

> Human beings, as self-aware beings and "I" bearers, are required to bring about their development in themselves through their own efforts. At a certain stage, they must be prepared to surrender whatever they have received from outside and to give birth, within their own self, to a higher "I." This higher "I" will not become hardened, but will enter a harmonious relationship with the entire world.[26]

If we believe that the purpose of educating a child is to fill them with content, then we have lost the understanding of what supports the health of a human being through adult life and into old age. The healthy adult maintains a learning relationship with the world. The healthy adult does not remain so separated that they become hardened and only wish to take in the parts of the outer world that validate their own inner life, their own sense of "me-self." However, even healthy adults who maintain a learning relationship with the world could find themselves full of content that has arisen from the humanly invented world.

Although we may appreciate nature and recognize the harmonizing effects it has on the human being, we are still far from recognizing the essential effects it has on the development of the good, the harmonious, and the true as the foundations for our inner life.

The kingdoms of nature, like the human body itself, are born out of a relationship to wisdom that lives beyond the capacity of the so-called human-made inventions. This wisdom is not just a content-based education for the human being, but it reminds us of who we are and why we are here—whether it be the awe we feel as we look up at the night sky, the harmony we feel in seeing the rolling green hills, the uplifting of the soul that we can experience from the vast blue sky, the power and strength that the mountains reflect to us, or the striving for light that the kingdom of plants reminds us of. The kingdoms of nature are the external harmonies of our internal laws.

As we emancipate ourselves from this original relationship to nature, we are left with the impressions of the human-made world. At the same time, nature itself is being dethroned from its kingly task of reminding us of the internal kingdoms within us.

Supporting the Living Nature of Learning

To experience this in the form of a simple exercise, take a large mirror and find a person, or some people, to practice this with. Center yourself by closing your eyes and quietly feeling into the activity of your inner life—don't focus on your thinking, but bring your awareness to your chest area and observe the quality of the inner activity within you.

Now look at the other person's reflection in the mirror for thirty seconds. Then turn and look directly at that person for the same length of time. And, again, go back to looking at their image in the mirror. Notice that the same "picture" produces a different inner activity depending on whether this picture is one of the living person, or rather an image or reflection of that person.

Of course, we as adults can bring inner activity to this image from out of ourselves, through our own efforts. But when we are left strictly with what is produced by the reality of the person before us in contrast to what is produced by the *image* of the reality of that person—this amounts to a significant difference for our inner life. The mirror can give me information, but the living reality gives so much more.

The heart of genuine education for children is to teach them *how to learn*: the process of learning, and how to develop and strengthen independent learning capacities. This is still done through content, but content that is delivered in a soul-connected way out of the teacher's capacities of thinking, feeling, and acting. It cannot be given merely as "recipe information" to be memorized, but must be given as content that feeds the child's deeper soul forces, their inner capacity to think, to feel, and to will. True education awakens them to their *capacity* to think, feel, and act, and not only to increase the *content* of thinking, feeling, and willing. It is impossible for a computer, serving in the role of teacher, to develop in its students the *capacity* to freely think, because the computer's "thinking" is itself developed through the *content* of thought.

What follows is an excerpt from a sample lesson given by Rudolf Steiner to first grade teachers; try to see how the experience of learning through the life processes comes to expression here, and what insights you can gain from this.

> You need not hesitate, quite early on, to take out a box of paints and set a glass of water beside it (indeed, it is a good idea to conduct such lessons quite soon with the children). After you have pinned white paper to the blackboard with drawing tacks, you take up a brush, dip it in the water and then into the paint, and make a small yellow patch on the white surface. When you have finished, you let each child come to the blackboard and make a similar small patch. Each patch must be separate from the others so that in the end you have several yellow patches.
>
> Then you dip your brush into the blue paint and put blue next to your yellow patch. And you let the children come up and put on the blue in the same way. When about half of them have done this, you say, "Now we shall do something else; I am going to dip my brush in the green paint and put green next to the other yellow patches." Avoiding as well as you can making them jealous of one another, you let the remaining children put on the green in the same way. All this will take time, and the children will digest it well. It is indeed essential to proceed very slowly, taking only a very few small steps in the lesson.

> The time then comes for you to say, "I am going to tell you something that you will not yet understand very well, but one day you will understand it quite well. What we did at the top, where we put blue next to the yellow, is more beautiful than what we did at the bottom, where we put green next to the yellow." This will sink deeply into the children's souls. It will be necessary to return to this thought several times, but they will also puzzle away at it themselves. They will not be entirely indifferent to it but will learn to understand quite well from simple, naïve examples how to feel the difference between something beautiful and something less beautiful.[27]

Imagine that the lesson described above was produced over the Internet, with children just watching the lesson on a screen. Even *reading* this lesson can bring up all sorts of intellectual objections. Instead of us *experiencing* the reality that yellow and blue do indeed produce in the human soul an objective inner activity of greater harmony than that produced by yellow and green, we think he is leaving the children unfree—telling them what to think. We may think, "Who can tell anyone else what is beautiful or not?" But if we *live* the lesson, we can recognize that it speaks beyond the level of the information contained in it.

Through the capacity to think, I can think the truth. Because the capacity of thinking is born out of the true, it recognizes the true and feels at home in it. Through the capacity to feel, I can feel the harmonious, and through the capacity to will, I can do the good. These capacities exist within the child, but they need to be unfolded through the child's relationship to the surrounding world. When a teacher expresses true, harmonious, and good content, this supports the child's willing participation.

Primary school children need to be educated by teachers who present content of the true, the harmonious, and the good to support the process of awakening individually to their capacities of thinking, feeling, and willing.

Through the ground of the life processes, these capacities allow for the development of true, independent learning. And through an individualized relationship to the life processes, each capacity is developed further.

The next real necessity of formal education is to teach a child *how to learn*, and, through our engaging with them, teach them to recognize what wants to live on in them. What lights up in their relationship to the world? What aspects of the outer world are they drinking in because they thirst for them?

Once we can identify what wants to live on within the child, we can guide and mentor individual children to support and awaken the right content for their future tasks.

> Somebody can understand their subjects of instruction completely; they can be a mine of information, but unfit to teach, because they do not know what streams out of the human being, what elicits the individuality of the other human being. Not until we refrain from rules and regulations and ask which human being is this, and put the best human being into the place where they are needed, will we fulfill the ideals in ourselves which [Anthroposophy] has brought.[28]

What is important is not only what we know, in terms of the content of information we carry, but who we are and the quality of our deeper soul capacities. We are under an illusion if we think that those who possess an abundance of information content about a particular profession are fit for the task of carrying out that profession well. For instance, think of how many people are educated in the field of medicine because of its standing in the world, and yet medicine does not fit with the nature of all those individuals. The more we think that "good medicine" has less to do with the human being practicing it and more to do with the information that the human being carries, the sooner artificial intelligence will dominate this profession.

To begin with, learning takes place unconsciously through the life processes, but we can awaken the capacity for independent learning if we can understand how to utilize the life processes as we teach the required content. The life processes can also be understood in terms of how we learn and grow through all our encounters in the external world around us. However, in formal education we sometimes recognize barriers to being able to pass certain thresholds and truly grasp hold of the world in an individual way.

From age six all the way to age fourteen, the child is primarily required to be taught what is true and right to learn, and in doing so, to *learn how to learn fully* during school time. In order for the child to develop the independent learning capacity that is essential for high school, they need to be able to go through all the steps of the life processes; and in the realm of formal learning, these life processes can be separated out and supported. The learning steps follow the same digestive pathway through the seven life processes—but they can be named differently, in order to reflect how they work in the context of learning. In this way, they are designated as follows:

>Perceiving
>Relating
>Assimilating
>Individualizing
>Practicing
>Growing
>Creating

Just as we have three thresholds of digestion that need to be crossed before we can truly individualize and re-create our bodies anew, we likewise have three thresholds that need to be crossed in order for the outer lessons to become an inner content. The first threshold is the threshold of the senses. If the child does not have a healthy development of the senses, then conscious learning through the life processes becomes very challenging. The senses provide the foundations of the capacities for *attention, self-regulation*, and *healthy attachment* that are required to begin formal learning.

Without these three foundations born from the care and development of the twelve senses especially in the first seven years of life, there will be a limitation to the function of the three thresholds of learning. Instead of the child being able to take in the world, they will be distracted from the right *perceptions*—perceptions that bring us into *relationship* with the content.

The next threshold is our ability to *assimilate* the content once we have related to it. Most educational testing requirements of the modern world are not interested in going beyond the process of assimilation, preferring instead that the child simply regurgitate what has been given to them. The child who can only regurgitate is limited in their ability to approach the following, third threshold. The third threshold is when the child is at risk of eliminating too quickly what they have taken in, and the knowledge may go in and out of them without their being able to *individualize* it.

Just as with the twelve senses—where we can recognize the individual expression of the hyper and hypo senses in the child which allows us to engage individually with that person—the seven life processes reveal to us what the child wants to take in and what they find difficult to take in, digest, and assimilate. If we can understand how human beings individually learn in the context of the seven life processes, then we can perceive and assess what the individual child wants to learn. At the same time, we can support the areas of difficulty that the child is experiencing and work through those difficulties.

In the healthy expression of the life processes, we begin to see what children take in as individuals and make their own. We begin to recognize this extraordinary relationship between what is outside the children and what can penetrate to their inner world. We begin to see the individual strengths of each child.

The adolescent can then head into high school as an independent learner. From this point on, our main education of the young person is aimed at developing the capacities further through fostering their strengths and working toward providing them with opportunities that enable them to see how their strengths and the strengths of others combine to maintain, develop, and create the world.

The adolescent's experience extends beyond the class community as its main educator—and, accordingly, the educational experience now needs to be fostered by the wider school community, beyond the school premises. This is the adolescent's first opportunity to consciously give back to the community the strengths of their individualized soul.

In the primary classroom, we are always faced with children at varying levels of learning capacity. We have the first group, who are predominantly still working through the senses, even though they are in primary school. They continue to need support with their sensory development and the balancing of their senses. They still find it quite difficult to learn in a content-based way. They often struggle with attention, self-regulation, or healthy attachment, all of which are needed in their relationship to the teacher, to the content, and to the class community as a whole in order for learning to be fruitful.

We then have the second group: the assimilating learners of the class. They can take in, relate, and assimilate what is given to them. They can regurgitate everything that has been taught to them. It appears as though they are learning, but they are not fully individualizing what has been taken in. They have developed a healthy gateway to the world by means of the senses. They can take in, relate, and assimilate

Supporting the Living Nature of Learning

what is being taught, but they have not yet learned to think independently or make the content truly their own.

The third group can individualize the content; they can individually take hold of the content. However, they advance their learning through *practice* and through developing faculties that allow them to express their individualized understanding. They can express *in a new way* to their class community what they have made their own.

By perceiving what lives in each child we may also recognize that, in a certain subject, one child may be able to individualize more readily than another—whereas in another subject, a different child can more readily individualize the content. These variations give us an insight into what "lights up" each individual soul.

The class community has to work together. The teacher cannot focus only on one group of learners, as the rest of the class will then remain unmet by the learning culture. However, if the teacher can recognize these three levels of learning then the teacher can create an opportunity for the class, as a community, to have their needs met. For instance, the "individualized learner" can be encouraged by the teacher to create exercises and activities that will facilitate the "individualized learners" to support the "sense learners," who are still predominantly working through their senses. In this way, the so-called advanced learners can give their individual gifts to the so-called beginning learners of the class.

This "community learning," lived out in the classroom, is the foundation for our capacity of working with others in the future. Those who have the capacity to individualize what they have learned *grow* further by supporting the growth of others within the community who need support. Without the opportunity to support the growth of the other, the "advanced student's" own growth would also be limited. In this way, the community grows together, and each member participates in the growth of the other.

As the child develops, they develop a relationship between their "me"—the everyday self—and the world that surrounds them. As the individual grows on into adulthood and continues to learn from the world, they are primarily growing more and more in terms of the "me." The senses unfold a direct and necessary experience of the duality of self and other, whereas the life processes develop the necessary content of "me," the everyday self.

The everyday self is absolutely essential for human development at this time. However, at a certain point, when we have grown into adulthood, we may find ourselves only perceiving what we want to perceive, only relating to the things we want to relate to, only assimilating the things that are in alignment with our personal preferences. This eventually limits and hardens us.

To continue our development as adults today we are required to individualize our learning. This is also a necessity in order to transform what lives in us. If we do not individualize what we have learned, then when we give back to the world what lives in us, we give back only what we were given, regurgitating what was once fed to us. In this way, we will only reproduce the community that once produced us. If we individualize our learning and transform what we have learned into something more, then we will produce a community that has progressed and evolved.

The last several decades have seen dramatic changes in outer human progress. The way we live together as human beings, and our awareness of health and education, have shifted exponentially. Technology has played a major role in these changes; it has changed, to an unprecedented degree, the way we interact, the way we learn, and the choices we make. Because of the currently common persuasive effects and advertising of social media, our feeling of needing to think for ourselves is steadily diminishing. With the rise of "internet connectivity," we are being influenced not only collectively, but personally, as the influences are being tailored to our personal preferences. These methods are amplifying the habits of the everyday self, and, in turn, decreasing the activity of the true, independent individuality.

> As long as human beings seek only for the satisfaction of their needs, they are personalities. If they exceed this, they are individualities.[29]

The rise of the so-called attention economy—in which apps (applications), the internet, and information are shaped around advertising and trying to influencing people's choices—is amplifying the dominion of personal preference. It is a technology-driven approach fueled by the personal preferences of others: namely, the financial gain and power of corporations and their shareholders. We may ask the question: "Was it the intention of the inventors in certain aspects of technology that these technologies would have such a strong impact on the healthy development of community and human lives?" One answer, as quoted by a former Facebook engineer, is: "[It is] very common for humans to develop things with the best of intentions, and for them to have unintended, negative consequences."[30] Many people would say that they had no idea the technology they created would have changed human habits in a way so detrimental to the wider society, right down to the school community of the classroom and even family life.

However, when they gather at the so-called habit summits to learn how to create devices and apps that elicit from us our time and energy and attention—what is termed "behavioral design" or "persuasive design" by the social technology industry—we cannot help but think that some of them know exactly what they are doing.[31] As a former Google strategist who helped build the matrix system for the company's global search advertising business, stated in a recent interview: "The attention economy incentivizes the design of technologies that grab our attention.... In doing so, it privileges our impulses over our intentions.... The dynamics of the attention economy are structurally set up to undermine the human will."[32] He, among others, is deeply concerned about the effect of technology not only on the individual will, but also on the functioning of democracy itself: "If politics is an expression of our human will, on individual and collective levels, then the attention economy is directly undermining the assumptions that democracy rests on."[33]

Studies have already proven (and further studies continue to prove) that the use of the internet and its games negatively affects the way a child thinks and feels—that is, as long as we still recognize empathy and attentiveness as positive attributes. But our society and our communities are being built from below up. They are built on economics and politics rather than healthy culture and human ennoblement.

There have been warnings. Back in 1951, Emil Bock wrote:

> It is generally assumed that through technical progress which, of course, is the fruit of the material science, we shall be able to live more "human" lives. The reverse is true. We are in danger of dropping to the animal level. If we are honest we must admit that with the magnificent progress of technical science, we have really increased our trouble and decreased our time. Our technical achievements have begun to recoil on us—to begin with, on our nerves. What was intended to alleviate life, in fact compels us to live in subhuman, mechanized conditions.[34]

How can we, the people—the consumers that the internet corporations target—come to an experience of knowing what we are leading ourselves, our families, and our communities into when we integrate these technology-based habits into our lives?

This development affects not only the realm of technology; in other essential aspects of society, such as the field of medicine, methods are also being developed by industries seeking to gain great profits. This can be seen in situations where overarching decisions have been made regarding prescriptive health guidelines—for example, the decision to reduce the standard "healthy blood pressure rate" so that far more individuals would need to be on prescribed medicines in order to reduce their blood pressure in accordance with that "new" rate. This decision was made by a board in which several members have financial interests in the pharmaceutical company that supplies the medicine in question.[35]

> This synthetic civilization must recoil upon us, because we are beings with soul and spirit, and we need a truly human environment to live in.[36]

Could we have known that medicine would have become an industry oriented more toward earning money than it is toward caring for the health and wellbeing of society—or even worse, an industry that knowingly increases the need for unnecessary and health-deteriorating synthetic medications or addictive opioid drugs in the name of better financial returns? The money is not being directed to healing the sick, but to medicating the healthy, because it is possible to achieve greater returns by getting all people on medication than it is by curing the relatively few sick people. Along with this, there is the realm of so-called smart drugs, which upgrade the human brain for a competitive edge. Medicine is heading further in the direction of the prioritization of money over health.

> Everything connected with medicine will make a great advance in the materialistic sense. People will acquire instinctive insights into the medicinal properties of certain substances and certain treatments—and thereby do terrible harm. But the harm will be called useful. A

> sick person will be called healthy, for it will be perceived that the particular applied treatment leads to something pleasing. People will actually *like* things that make human beings—in a certain direction—unhealthy.[37]

The community forms of the past are failing us, simply because many such forms are now based on the direction and guidance of policies driven by global corporations that seek profit and power over the health and wellbeing of the planet and its inhabitants. We cannot return to reproducing the community handed down to us by the past, unconsciously given to us—because we as a collective humanity have now progressed to the ability to individualize our ideals and to participate in community life independently, as creative individuals. But are we prepared to go up against the new forms of community arising through the dominance of materialism?

As this world continues on the path of materialism, the responsibility for the future rests in the hands of those individuals who choose to work together to create new community forms. Forms based not on the conventional aspects of the material world, but on new spiritual impulses, which must now be acquired through individuals.

> If only the old impulses were to continue to have an influence, the future prospect would inevitably be one where, to an unprecedented degree, technology of a purely external kind will not only overpower and outwardly overwhelm human beings but will paralyze them and take them over even to the point of utter destruction, because it will drive from the human soul everything of a religious, scientific, philosophical, and artistic nature and also any kind of higher moral feeling. People

will be something like living automatons if new spiritual impulses are unable to take hold.[38]

The greatest difficulty we face is that we stand at a place in our evolution where the old community forms are being eroded, but the healthy, new community forms have not yet developed. We have entered into a kind of chaos that requires us to be guided forward by the higher "I." New community forms will be developed out of individuals who are awakening to new spiritual impulses within themselves. Such individuals have their own direct relationship to the spiritual world through the spirit that dwells within, the awakened higher "I."

In the past, we were born into communities formed by religious or spiritual laws and values. Now we are born into a world directed by laws and values that are related more to greed and vanity than to spiritual principles. We cannot go backwards to the state in which we were unconsciously held and supported by spiritual laws and values. Therefore, the challenge we face today is: how can we consciously create anew our relationship to spiritual laws and values?

It is essential for new community to be evolved out of free, independent, individual beings who can choose to work together in order to implement what they have ascertained out of themselves: the spiritual insights and values that they wish to bring into the world around them. Between the breakdown of the old community and the development of the individuality that is mature enough to create with the spirit, a void has opened up through which diverting and destructive materialistic forces have taken hold.

We stand in need of individual, adult development of the higher "I" and independent capacities to think for ourselves; otherwise we will not be able to create communities that can reflect healthy development for all. The right care and development during childhood gives individuals the best means to develop themselves later in life.

The only way forward for community, and therefore for humanity as a whole, is for individuals to develop themselves and awaken to the capacities that will allow them, through working with others, to develop the world. If we continue to sleep into this future, then we will continue on a path of destruction. The call to awakening that now sounds in the modern "desert" of spiritual life touches the deepest recesses of our individual hearts. What will we choose to put our energy toward—a future that is self-serving, or a future that serves the whole?

The fact is that the basis of healthy care and development of the nervous system and senses in childhood supports this first and essential step of adult inner development. It is imperative for us to perceive the direction we are headed in as we make choices in our individual, family, and community lives about the increasing encroachment of technology upon early childhood—technologies that we know play a significant role in disturbing the healthy development of the senses in children. Deeply concerned teachers are recognizing that it is increasingly difficult to support the living process of learning in children who have already been affected by these community changes. These changes are leading the task of the classroom toward being a therapeutically focused challenge rather than allowing teachers to get on with the task of pedagogy.

The senses are not only essential for the initial awareness of the second self, but they are also essential for the second stage of education that children must embark upon if they are to learn actively in school and from life itself. If we adulterate the life processes by not teaching children how to think, but rather filling them with preferred content, then we do not support the development of independent individuals—rather, we train children to think what we want them to think. In a healthy world, this would not pose such a grave danger. But in a world filled with increasing corruption, we must teach children how to be incorruptible.

As we stand at the threshold of the necessity to awaken to our next steps in human development—not only in a few chosen individuals, but in the many—we begin to recognize that an increased experience of the separate self, of being "full of ourselves," could lead us away from the awakening of our higher "I." We will begin to see that what once began as a gift of our human experience—having a personal, separate sense of self in the sensory world—may well become a form of imbalance without the necessary step forward in transformation. If it comes to such an extreme point, then it will be difficult to differentiate the experience of selfhood from the list of traits commonly associated with narcissism.

Supporting the Living Nature of Learning

It is said that narcissism is currently the fastest growing diagnosis as a human psychological condition. Sigmund Freud coined the term *narcissism* in the 1950s, although "narcissistic personality disorder" was not recognized in the *Diagnostic and Statistical Manual of Mental Disorders* (DSM) until 1994. A list of traits, signs, and symptoms of the narcissist are all too common today in many world leaders—including leaders of corporations—who have extraordinary power over decisions concerning the future health and wellbeing of society.

The following is a list of the most common expressions of narcissism:

An obvious self-focus in interpersonal exchanges
An exaggerated sense of self-importance
Feeling hurt and rejected easily
A sense of entitlement, and requiring constant, excessive admiration
A lack of psychological awareness
Superiority, specifically toward people perceived as "lower" in status
Problems distinguishing the self from others
Difficulty maintaining healthy and satisfying relationships
Exploiting others for personal gain
Being preoccupied with fantasies about success, power, brilliance, beauty, or the perfect mate
Hypersensitivity to any insults or imagined insults
Behaving in an arrogant or haughty manner, coming across as conceited, boastful, and pretentious
Inability to admit wrongdoing
Exaggerating achievements, abilities, and talents

- Vulnerability to shame rather than guilt
- Expecting special favors and unquestioning compliance with their expectations
- Monopolizing conversations and belittling or looking down on people they perceive as inferior
- Insisting on having the best of everything—for instance, the best car or office
- Haughty body language
- Expecting to be recognized as superior even without achievements that warrant it
- Flattery toward people who admire and affirm them
- Detesting those who do not admire them
- Severe anger if orders or directions are not followed by others
- Only associate with equally special people
- Expecting constant praise and recognition for achievements
- Denial of remorse and gratitude
- Unrealistic goal setting
- Using other people without considering the cost of doing so
- Pretending to be more important than they actually are
- Inability to view the world from the perspective of other people
- Inability to listen to others
- Bragging and exaggerating, taking pride in their achievements and those of their family
- Claiming to be an "expert" at many things
- A strong desire for control over relationships
- Social withdrawal
- Lacking empathy, especially for perceived weaknesses
- Being envious of others and believing that others envy them

Supporting the Living Nature of Learning

- Obsession and envy toward those perceived as being of a higher status
- A distant, practical attitude with regard to personal relationships
- Increased risk of using drugs and alcohol
- Lack of awareness regarding others
- Can "write off" friends permanently over small or imagined issues

Narcissism comes from the character Narcissus in the Greek myth of the young man who falls in love with himself—falling deeply in love with all the things that he admires in himself. However, Narcissus is not presented to us as a singular figure, but he is presented along with the story of the nymph Echo.

The myth of Echo is the story of a very talkative nymph. Others admire Echo for her voice. The goddess Venus especially admires her magnificent voice and song. Zeus was frolicking with the nymphs, as he commonly did, and Echo set out to distract his wife Hera (Juno) so that Zeus (Jupiter) could escape her sight. Echo was stalling Hera through incessant talking, trying to convince her that her husband was in the city and not where she suspected, that is, frolicking with the nymphs. As a punishment for her trickery, Hera curses Echo by making her able to only *finish* another's sentence, but unable to start one—and further, unable to say anything of her own. Hera diminished Echo's capacity of communicating her own thoughts so that she could only repeat the last words of what another had said. An echo of sound, in the sense of an aural effect, was named after her.

Echo falls in love with Narcissus when she sees him at a distance, while he is chasing frightened deer into his traps. This love grows ever deeper for Echo, admiring Narcissus without his knowledge.

Narcissus, tired from hunting and from the heat, takes a rest by a pool of spring water. Thirsty from his work, he begins to drink; seeing his own reflection, he becomes captivated by the image of the beauty he has seen in the pool. His thirst now grows for that image, and he falls deeply in love with himself.

Echo continues to watch Narcissus secretly, but eventually her presence and love is exposed to Narcissus; but Narcissus rejects her love, preferring to love himself. Echo, heartbroken, prays to Venus, who, compassionately it seems, makes Echo slowly disappear in form—but she must remain as a voice and be heard by all in her affliction of being unable to say anything out of herself, but able only to echo what others have said.

Not recognizing his error, Narcissus cannot quench this new thirst and he eventually wastes away with this unquenchable love for himself. He mimics Echo's diminishing power, and in place of his being, the "narcissus flower" now develops. This flower is still found near river banks, so that it can be reflected in the water. These gifts of each—of Echo and Narcissus—are left behind for humanity; by means of them, we can remember their fates, reminding us not to misuse the capacities given to us by using them against others or by falling in love with ourselves.

The narcissists generally get the bad press. But narcissists are only able to grow as strong as they do because of the "echoists" hidden in those people who allow them this power. We see people using their time and energy against the healthy development of others by echoing what the narcissists tell them. Rather than thinking for themselves and being productive themselves, they copy others and go along with the lies. Forsaking the work of developing further through individual capacities, the echoists allow themselves to be ruled by the narcissists.

The condition of the "echoist"—the passive repeater of official, unquestioned opinions or of "public opinion"—may well become so destructive in its prevalence as to warrant identification as a new psychological disorder, though we may not use that term for it. Instead of learning how to think for ourselves, we echo back the opinions of others, and follow the nudges the corporations consistently give to our will without our free thinking or choice. Instead of individualizing our capacity of thinking, our thinking becomes a shadow of its potential.

In the age of the greatest egotism, we can understand this rise of narcissism within society as an individual issue. We can name individuals in places of power in our community who are narcissistic. We're also faced with narcissistic companies, narcissistic corporations, and narcissistic governments. But can we see where the echoists are contributing to this? Even if we can see that it is the will of those narcissistic corporations to persuade us, we should also ask ourselves: Do we put effort into not being persuaded?

We, in ourselves, may not identify with these extremes of narcissism and echoism; but we can find these two tendencies within ourselves and within others whenever we get caught in the personal drama of the "me-self"—the drama of thinking that leads to the polar extremes of either "I am everything" or "I am nothing." We can also recognize that both of these traits—"narcissism" and "echoism"—can live simultaneously within the soul of each person. However, one of them generally gains the upper hand when we become stuck in one pole of the imbalance—even though the other trait is just as problematic in causing the one-sidedness.

But we do not need to remain stuck. In fact, these two polar traits can help us to recognize how we need to work in order to reach our larger aim of freeing ourselves.

With a simple clay exercise, we can perceive how we can find a balancing force or "balancer" through these two one-sided tendencies—a balancer that can help us to see our unconscious tendencies and to learn from them. This is a great exercise for bringing movement into areas where we feel stuck, caught, or bound by our own inner processes.

Supporting the Living Nature of Learning

THE INDIVIDUAL THREEFOLD EXERCISE IN CLAY

- The materials required are three fist-sized pieces of clay, a pen, and paper.
- Identify the issue or struggle you wish to explore. This could be a relationship issue, an internal struggle, or a community/world issue.
- With the first piece of clay, create a gesture that represents this issue or struggle for you. Once created, the clay gesture will be a very personal representation of what you have identified as the issue you want to explore through the exercise.
- Name the gesture of the clay and record it on the paper. Again, how you name the gesture will be personal only to you and need only have meaning for you. This first gesture will have feelings of both discomfort and biographical familiarity attached to it.
- We now want to find the gesture that is *polar opposite* to this first gesture. Be aware that our tendency is to first seek the *solution* to the first gesture, but this is not what we want. The polarity to gesture 1 will also be uncomfortable, and once you find it, you will recognize its familiarity within your biography.
- Name gesture 2 on the same piece of paper.
- Beneath the names of gesture 1 and gesture 2, write a list of five disadvantages of being in each of these states. To achieve this, just imagine yourself in the state and list what you experience as being the negative elements of being caught in that state.
- Then write a list, under each gesture, of five advantages of being in each state. This is more difficult to do than writing the disadvantages of the state, as we have initially identified each state from a negative perspective. With persistence, you will find that each of these states does also have within it elements that are, or that can become, strengths or advantages within us. You may find that within your lists, some items are both

advantages and disadvantages, and end up on both lists; this is normal.
- Place the gestures in front of you: one to the left and one to the right. You may notice that the gestures constitute a polarity not only in terms of their qualities, but also in terms of their form. These gestures represent the two poles of a state that you are immersed in or facing. One gesture will pull you toward egotism, and one gesture will pull you toward a "lack of a sense of self," a diminished feeling of self. Should you get deeply drawn into one of the polar qualities, it may flip you to the other side of the polarity, and vice versa. As long as there is no resolution, this oscillation will continue. The resolution resides in what follows. Knowing that these polarities pull you from egotism (full of self) to a diminished sense of self, and back again, what is the balance between them?
- With the third piece of clay, create a gesture of this balance. Finding this balance may take some time and contemplation, but it is there and you will recognize it when it comes. Sometimes this third gesture has elements of gestures 1 and 2.
- Name this third gesture.
- Now describe how you will incarnate this balance into your life so that the pole of egotism ("I am everything") and the pole of diminished self ("I am nothing") lose their grip over time. It is useful to note that, should you get caught in one polar quality in the future, you can return to balance by picking up the advantages of the opposite polar quality, and vice versa.
- Now go back to your original issue. Has anything changed in terms of how you experience the issue or in terms of your attitude toward it?
- It may be useful to retain the pieces of clay for a period of time in order to remind yourself of the process you are working on and will continue to work on.

The error of one-sidedness can awake the "balancer," or middle. The individualized will then knows exactly what to work upon within ourselves.

We would like to think that "children will change the future"; but the reality is that children rely on the adults within the community to make decisions that will allow them to grow up in a healthy way, so that they can participate in the progress of humanity when they, too, reach adulthood. It is adults who guide the greater decisions within the lives of our communities. Throughout all areas of human health, cultural wellbeing, and evolutionary progress, we are now being more and more led by individuals who govern political parties, corporations, and industries, and who have proven to not place the health and wellbeing of humanity, and of the individuals who comprise it, as their main priority. We are being misled and deceived by a mindset that prioritizes financial gain and power over others above the health and wellbeing of humanity and of the world we live in.

This deception has been long in the making, and often under the guise of progress for all; and presently it continues through the very ideologies that have created a situation of inequality where one percent of humanity owns more than half the world's wealth.

> Everywhere you can see how things are being arranged in a way that makes people less and less inclined to take truthfulness into account.[39]

Individuals working consciously with inner development cannot sidestep the forces working in the collective consciousness of their community, but rather they must first encounter these forces within themselves. If it is there, in the collective experience, it will also be there in my own being. It may be present in the form of a particular personal expression, but we have to encounter it as a part of our self-transformation.

Through the inner development path, we take upon ourselves exercises that will usurp the "me-self" and strengthen the capacities of the higher "I." This is necessary, because if we do not take this step, we will find ourselves immersed in the feeling of despair that so many individuals are facing today.

Many people are not asleep to their personal patterns and habits of thinking and feeling; they are awake to them. Very many individuals today have awakened the beginnings of the higher "I," the results of which enable them to witness the errors of the ways of life in the external world around them—but more essentially, the qualities of erroneous thinking, feeling, and will impulses that live on within their own being.

This is the difficulty that faces everyone on this genuine path. The witness can look within at the erroneous thoughts, feelings, and impulses of will; but the individual does not necessarily distinguish them as "other," and may in fact perceive them as the self. This flawed awareness, instead of illuminating our lives toward the spirit, then makes the soul feel depressed, hopeless, anxious, and lacking in self-esteem. This is quite contradictory to the qualities of the narcissist. But it is especially here where we need to guard against retreating into inwardly becoming the echoist, who has no individual voice.

As we awaken to the higher "I"—the bearer of our individual ideals and our individualized will impulses—we see how vast is the darkness in which this small light shines.

These patterns—the stories—that once were outside me, are now seen to be inside me. The everyday self has overidentified with the content of its own inner world, which it received through the education of its surrounding community. The awakened "I" must build upon itself, upon the true self, so that it is possible to begin to reorient one's identity from the everyday self to the true "I."

The first transformation that individuals take upon themselves as a task in our time is to transform the world: a "world" once outside, which is now inside—the "world" of thoughts and habits that the everyday self has absorbed in the course of its education. In fact, we can say that the piece of "world" that I can "raise up" is right where I am. It is not something I have to go looking for, to go out searching for; it is something that exists within me. To transform what was once outside me (and which I now perceive to be inside me) is my first task. The mystery of why certain things, once outside, are now inside this particular being that I call "me," is a part of the great mystery of karma. It is also therefore a part of the potential for developing the spiritual self: the "spiritual body" formed through my transforming of my particular inner world.

This does not mean we do not work vigorously at developing the world; but only that we must recognize that the first part of the world in need of development is the part of the world I have within me. I must find a way of transforming the patterns of this thinking, this feeling, and these will impulses that belong to a world in decline—I must find a way of raising them up, engaging them with content that flows from the spiritual world itself. This becomes the individual's greatest possibility of awakening their individual spiritual strengths. It is through the individualized will that this becomes possible. By engaging this will into our thinking, new thoughts arise instead of patterned, abstract thinking.

When we take our inner world *personally* instead of objectively and responsibly, then we miss out on partaking in the renewed strength streaming toward us from the spirit.

My inner life is a host to all of the other consciousnesses that were once outside me; my own seed form of the spirit self within me allowed those particular external consciousnesses to enter and make their impressions upon me. By transforming what is now inside me, I start to transform the world around me. A new stage of the life processes begins as we further spiritualize the world. The first stage was the digestion of earthly substance; then, receiving the environment through its impressions; and finally, transforming the results of those impressions by means of the individualized will.

What you seek is also seeking you.[40]

The greatest of difficulties are now being faced by the many people who are waking up to an ability to witness

Supporting the Living Nature of Learning

"all that lives in me." This witnessing capacity does not fully arise until adulthood. However, many young people, even from their sixteenth or seventeenth years onward, are already aware of most of the errors of their thinking. But they are not yet able to recognize the origin or source of this erroneous thinking, and such a realization often demoralizes them. Their feeling life becomes a bombardment of self-hatred and loathing because of their awareness of the false inner world that they carry: an inner world that has been impressed upon them by the community conditioning around them. An inner world that is instilled into them by the greed of corporations—those that want to persuade them to believe that they need to buy things, or to be someone other than who they are in order to be acceptable to the world. An inner world that is being sculpted and formed by technologies, behind which lives a consciousness that believes in gain only for the few. Immorally directed technology is infringing upon their inner world, imprinting itself and persuading them to think certain things.

All kinds of self-harm, eating disorders, drug use, and degrading sexuality occur through the lack of self-respect that arises due to a full or partial recognition of these errors of our own inner world. We find ourselves so far away from the airbrushed ideal of being a person worthy of "trending." And yet, genuine witnessing is the first glimpse of our ability to free ourselves from the delusion of wanting to be an artificial person.

We have to take hold of our patterns of thinking, our judgments, our criticisms, and our ideas of what is right and wrong that have been handed down to us. We have to use this "other," which I have now called "me"—the "otherness" of all that I have internalized from the erroneous thinking of the world—and through the awakened individualized will, we must work with effort toward the truth, harmony, and goodness of human life and human potential.

The primary school child has "learned how to learn" through utilizing the life processes and through learning to think individually. In educating high school students, we now have the task of teaching them how to extend this capacity. They learn that their capacities can be extended through their ability to learn greater content from the world by means of the life processes. In becoming capable, through the world, of independently expanding their capacities of thinking, feeling, and will intentions, they can thereby, through learning independently, "grow themselves up." The heart and core of high school is to awaken in the students a realization of the fact that through their capacity for independent learning, their other capacities will grow.

Between the ages of fourteen and twenty-one, our main task is to support the individual in their process of awakening and developing their own capacities. This requires them to have a capacity for independent learning, which should have been established in the primary school years through the life processes. Each young person can be supported in developing independence in their inner world of thoughts, feelings, and will intentions. We can help them to develop their own opinions out of themselves, and to

Supporting the Living Nature of Learning

begin meeting the world on the basis of their independent, inner assessment.

Because of the new self-consciousness that arises as the thinking capacity awakens within the fourteen- and fifteen-year-old, the adolescent at this time often has an uncomfortable awakening in relation to themselves and the world around them. Even if they never speak it out, they carry deeper questions than what they can show in their behavior—deeper questions than they can even formulate within themselves in order to express to others. They live with a feeling of insecurity about what is "normal"; they are in a perpetual state of wondering, "Am I normal?" This shows us that their thinking, as a capacity, can now be developed from out of their own individual selves.

The education necessary to bring adolescents at this age more harmoniously into the world must constitute a "bridging" between what lives in their souls as questions, and what the teacher can recognize and answer as a part of the education *without the adolescents having to ask the questions aloud.*

> If a student is unable to formulate a question which they experience inwardly, then the teacher must be capable of doing this themselves, so that the teacher brings about such a formulation in class; and the teacher must be able to satisfy the feeling that then arises in the students when the question comes to expression.[41]

We do not need to expose this feeling within them. The exposure of the feeling "I am not normal" in the adolescent is not useful to them within the school environment.

We no longer need to present content that unites them as a member of a particular community, but we must rather try to broaden their exposure to a variety of community expressions, allowing them to experience the attributes and qualities of all possible pathways. And we can do this through awakening their individual thinking in the context of coming to an understanding of the world around them. We are all individual, but the world is still lawful. Therefore, our thinking must learn to adapt itself to the intricate lawfulness of the world. This prevents them from falling into a tendency to parrot or echo, instead awaking their individual thinking.

This lawfulness is an expression of the spirit in the world. Here, we can help the adolescents to wake up to this spirit in the world and to the various kingdoms of nature through which it expresses itself, so that they may find peace in their very normal "not normal" inner experiences.

We may want to stuff teenagers full of the ideologies that we carry. But in reality, awakening to their own point of view is what will lead them to the awakening of their individual ideals. This is then the instrument of their own striving: the capacity for independent thinking that lives behind the content of what they need to learn.

Presenting opposing points of view to teenagers allows them to have the greatest freedom in developing their own capacity to think. Exposing them to diversity is useful in allowing them to find themselves within varying points of view. As their educators, we can help the adolescents by assessing the one-sidedness of the community at large; this enables us to see what is living in the adolescents' own thoughts and feelings as one-sided impressions from the community. From here, we can recognize the actual diversity of life that is not yet represented to them through their education, and from here we can take the initiative to include this diversity in their education. If it is missing during those initial, formative teenage years and we only include it later on in life, then this will not help them to transform the effects of their past conditioning. But by exposing them to other points of view and allowing them to find for themselves "where they stand" at that given time, we are not cultivating fixed standpoints but rather attempting to awaken, through the experience of polarities, that which in them is individual.

By the time they are sixteen or seventeen years old, they are increasingly interested in the other's experiences. Rather than wanting to discover in which ways they themselves are normal or not normal, they now want to know what it is like to be in the shoes of the other. They are more accepting of the shoes they themselves wear, but they also know that unless they engage with the other, they will not journey far in exploring the world. They increase their feeling capacity, from out of themselves, through experiences of the world and of the other.

The eighteen- or nineteen-year-old is becoming aware that they can expand their own will capacity out of themselves; but they also recognize that, unfortunately, they may have very little will to do so. This expanding will capacity is especially hindered if they have been stuffed full of pessimistic images of the future of the world. "What subject you deal with is much less important than that you do not bring this debilitating pessimism to young people."[42] And, of course, this is not only true for the education of the high school student, but it is also true of the ongoing education of all individuals living in community.

There is a relentless movement toward supporting individual choices, individual desires, and individual lifestyles—and yet, we have to consider the fragmentation of community coherence that can occur if we have lost our relationship to the unifying spirit. Are there laws in the spiritual world according to which we can test the truth or goodness of our individual choices? Or do the criteria of all our individual choices come down to nothing more than our personal preferences?

> True love can be attained only if the soul is not hardened in separateness and plurality, but if it finds calm and peace in the true totality and in the whole spirit.[43]

Freedom of the individual is a necessity for building the community of the spirit. It is impossible to build a community of the spirit through unfree human beings. But we must recognize that this freedom arises out of the spiritual nature in ourselves. Supporting the true freedom of another is the beginning of supporting the awakening of the spirit within them.

The use of "recreational" consciousness-altering drugs serves to withdraw the higher "I." Many of these drugs can induce experiences that give the user a personal experience confirming that there is more to life than the everyday "me-self" consciousness. However, the path forward at this point in human evolution—the path leading to our next step in spiritual development—can only be taken in freedom and through our individual efforts. By their very nature, drugs that change your consciousness for you are opponents of this higher path, as they sidestep the inner strength that must be gained through conscious efforts at self-awakening. The necessity of this individually won strength may be difficult to understand from the perspective of our ordinary sensory world experience; but in the realms of spiritual activity, if we have not found our way there *out of our own inner strength*, then it will be impossible to inwardly govern ourselves in the face of further spiritual experiences and advancement. (For more on this, see my book *Living Inner Development*.[44]) This lays us open to many difficulties, including the spiritual deception of what may seem like liberation, but which in reality is the creation of, and the being bound to, a "mystical me-self." This "mystical me-self" comes in the place of what otherwise would be a working from our individualized spirit, which is the only truly free aspect of the human being.

Addiction puts to sleep and makes unconscious the erroneous patterns that have arisen in our consciousness. But addiction also exposes us to greater conditioning. It relieves the consciousness of the feeling of error, but it can do so only for a short time before the unconscious patterns arise again with strengthened force. Therefore, a greater amount of the substance is now required to once again "rise higher" above the experience of these unconscious patterns. Then the swing happens again, back to the erroneous patterns; but at a certain point, the "witness awareness" has withdrawn. Without the witness, it is impossible to distinguish what is self and what is other in the inner realms.

"Process addictions" (addictions that do not involve ingesting something but are formed by stimulated chemical release through reward triggers) are also attached to the need to block out the erroneous thought patterns. We seek the comfort provided by a consciousness other than our own. When we cannot tolerate the internal world or want reprieve from it, then we seek to soothe ourselves. When we try to "get outside of ourselves" by means of the various consciousness-altering methods—whether that be alcohol, marijuana, painkillers, and so on—or when we seek other process addictions—for example, computer games, gambling, sex, or pornography—then in either case, we are actually trying to nullify or soothe the experience of the erroneous patterns of thought within us.

> Renewal will be possible only if we face the destructive forces within ourselves.[45]

All of this, however, becomes a different problem for the development of both society and the individual when addiction has occurred within the child before they have awakened to the "witnessing self." Before the individual awakens to the ability to look upon their own inner life and to recognize it as not being one and the same as the "I"—before that age, all addiction is something inflicted upon the child through the surrounding community.

At a certain point in every individual's development, we gain the ability to see into ourselves; and this seeing is painful because we see everything that is not aligned with the spirit in us. It is impossible for the "I" to see the "I" from the earthly side of the spiritual threshold; and the "I" therefore cannot see all that belongs to itself. The "I" cannot see the fullness of the true, the harmonious, and the good that lives within the individual soul because these things in the soul belong to the "I"; however, the "I" does naturally see the errors and registers them as such. To a special degree, the adolescents stand in need of the help and support of their community, in order to see what in them is "on the right track."

Embarking upon a path of inner development is not an easy task, because you have to be able to bear the reality of what lives in human nature. Every individual will be horrified by the thoughts and feelings that live inside themselves, but we must know that they were once outside. For one reason or another, they now cling to you, and it is up to you to transform them.

We do not transform the erroneous thoughts and feelings by focusing on them as *errors in-and-of-themselves*; rather, we must recognize them and try to strive for the spiritual aspect of what they are becoming. Our own spiritual consciousness alone is worthy of leading us now. The more we heed its guidance, the more this consciousness will unfold its power to help us.

> This higher self now becomes the inner ruler who directs the circumstances of the outer self with sure guidance. As long as the outer self has the upper hand and control, this inner self is its slave and therefore cannot unfold its own powers.[46]

In order that we are able to usurp the "me" directing our lives, we must try to keep a watchful eye on the diversions it will likely throw in the path of our striving. What follows is a simple exercise that can help us to become conscious of the diverting tendencies that live within us as shadows of our intentions. This is a useful exercise in working on collective struggles and community issues that require the awareness of the group in order to find a progressive path forward.

The Threefold Community Exercise

- The group lists the issues it wants to deal with, and from this list decides on one or more issues that are to be the main priorities. Write down these main issues on separate pieces of paper, placing each in the center of a large table for the whole group to see.
- For this exercise, each member of the group will need three fist-sized pieces of clay, a pen, and paper.
- Taking one of the main issues identified by the group, each member of the group imagines their ideal response to the issue in the form of an individual activity. Individually, each person then creates a gesture—using one

Supporting the Living Nature of Learning

piece of clay—of their view of an ideal response. Once created, the clay gesture will be a personal representation of what you have identified as an ideal in response to the community issue.

- Each person names their gesture and places it in the center of the table, together with everyone else's gestures, around the related issue.
- Each person writes the name they have chosen on a label, and places the label beside their clay gesture. At this stage of the exercise, every individual should have their first gesture in the circle at the center of the table or room.
- Individually, each person now creates, with the second piece of clay, a gesture of what within their own self stands in the way or blocks the community ideal that they have created in gesture 1. This will be sensed as a negative or opposite expression to their first clay gesture.
- Upon further examination, it will be realized that this second gesture also represents a familiar pattern in one's own biography. Again, each person will have an individualized representation of their "block" to their own ideal embodied in gesture 1.
- Once you have completed gesture 2, give it a name (this is kept to yourself).
- With the third piece of clay, each individual now creates a gesture that stands in complete polarity to gesture 2. The polar gesture is more of a challenge to identify, as it is not the ideal again but the opposite or "negative" tendency. You will recognize the polar quality as it will also feel uncomfortable and will have a certain familiarity.
- Name gesture 3 (also keeping it to yourself).

- Place your two polar-related clay pieces—gestures 2 and 3—on the table, on each side of gesture 1. You will notice that one pole has an egotistic, "intensified sense of self" character and the other a "diminishing of self" character.
- The group is now free to examine the response to the issue that was chosen, and each individual can speak about their experience of the exercise as they feel inspired.

Questions that may arise within the group are:

What effect has the experience of doing the exercise had on the identified issue?
What is the effect on the individuals who are trying to discover and implement a community/group response?
How will this experience shape the community response?
How will this experience shape the individual response?

Through this exercise, we can discover what, ideally, each individual can strive toward out of their own freedom in order to support the issue; and when this is shared with others, it can uplift the quality of our working together. But I also come to realize the qualities in me that divert my intentions; and in knowing them, I can keep an eye on them. This part is not shared in the course of the exercise because it is my own to deal with, and no one else can keep an eye on it for me. We give our best selves to the community; and as for own our diversions, we must transform them ourselves.

The vast majority of human beings recognizes the necessity of human progress and that this progress takes its form in various ways. We generally use the word *progress* to describe what we have accomplished as human beings in the physical world—that is, the changes we have experienced in human civilization throughout the generations. Changes such as the quality of life, what is available to us, and the experiences that we can now have—these changes, we say, are the results of "human progress."

Progress in technology, medicine, and education are Western signatures of our evolution as humanity. However, it is the progress of consciousness that truly constitutes an expression of human evolution. If we create an extraordinary world of new technology, but we ourselves cultivate our impulses of greed and vanity or the need for power and possessions, then how much progress have we truly made? Our materialistic worldview does not recognize that the purpose of life is the evolution of consciousness.

Our first community arises from being born into a certain family. Or, it arises from gathering together with people who have common physical attributes. It arises out of people relating to each other out of common, earthly tendencies. The original community can be described as:

- A unified body of individuals, such as a state or commonwealth, or groups of people with common interests or living in a particular area.
- Broadly, it is an interacting population of various kinds of individuals (who can be seen as different "species") in a common location, a group of people with a common characteristic or a common interest in

living together within a larger society—for example, a community of retired persons, a monastic community, a group linked by a common policy, or a body of persons or nations having a common history or common social, economic, and political interests.
- It may also be a body of persons with common professional interests, scattered throughout a larger society—for example, the academic community, the scientific community, or people in society at large who share joint ownership of or participation in some common cause.

The new community that is now arising is one comprised of individuals freely working together to bring new spiritual impulses into the world around them. They may not feel united in community with the people who are their blood-bond family; they may not feel united in community with people who have similar physical attributes. The members of the new community may not have common interests and may not live in a particular area, sharing a common location; they may be different in their social, economic, and political interests; they may not have any joint ownership of possessions. But nevertheless, they are a community: a community of the spirit. The single sign uniting all individuals in the new community is that each will be working, in their own way, on the evolution of consciousness for the progress of humanity.

> There are in fact really only two possibilities for the future. One is that things will turn out to be in harmony with the evolution planned by the gods for humanity, and the other is the opposite.[47]

3

Our Individual Task toward Spirit-led Community

The awakening in daily life of the individualized will—the activity of the higher "I," which can only be accessed through participating in the duality of the sensory world—is the first step in our conscious spiritual development. This individualized will increases in strength and capacity through a consistent engagement of the will of the higher "I." In a practical sense, this process is often achieved through the will-filled thinking that emerges for those who are working toward truly thinking for themselves. It may not yet be recognized as a "spiritual" will, but it can certainly be seen as something different from the impulsive, unconscious, or conditioned forces that drive the everyday will.

Through ongoing efforts in inner development and meditation—especially through commitment to certain practices laid out in the guidance given about genuine inner training—a further experience of the higher "I"-awakening occurs in the form of the growing experience of an inner presence that is conscious of itself. A presence of an inner peace or an inner strength and stability whenever the individual turns their gaze inward is the quality of this second new experience within. This provides a resource that allows us to meet the world in such a way that we are less disturbed by the continual, restless impressions it makes. The third "I"-awakening is the birth of the higher "I" within the spiritual world. This awakening—an awakening to the reality of now being an individualized spiritual being within the higher worlds—is often referred to as the actual "birth of the higher 'I,'" even though the pre-awakenings can still be seen as stages of the higher "I"-experience leading up to this spiritual birth.

If, however, we wish to participate in the fruits of the spiritual world—regardless of the degree to which our higher "I" has already awakened—and to perceive the spirit in its living, expressed facets, then not only do we need to awaken the spirit within ourselves, but we must also build the capacities that allow us to perceive the workings of the spirit.

> If I now turn aside from every impression that can reach me from the surrounding physical world, I do not, when I look within, behold there a being that is totally inactive, but a being that is conscious of itself in a world of which I can know nothing as long as I only lay myself open to impressions that come to me through sense perception and through everyday thinking.[48]

The building of spiritual capacities for spiritual insight is necessary if the higher "I" is to be not only aware of itself in the spiritual world, but also aware of the consciousnesses that exist in the surrounding environment.

Our Individual Task toward Spirit-led Community

If we are to be able to realize our spiritual nature (our divine consciousness) within its home (the spiritual world), then this consciousness requires a body or sheath through which it can manifest as an individualized expression. The spiritual world does not provide this sheath for us. The spiritual world is a place in which the separated, ensouled "I"-consciousness does not come about of its own accord; rather, a certain spiritual "skin" must first be developed in order to serve as a vessel for the "I"-consciousness. Without this skin, we find ourselves—when in the spiritual world—in the vastness of consciousness, but with no knowledge of anything other than nothingness.

The human being has to develop a "skin"—the vehicle for independent spiritual life—through the transformation of their "counter-expression" (the everyday self) in the sensory world.

The outer sensory world is taken into us—becoming our inner content—by means of the life processes. As adults, this outer sensory world is expressed as the "everyday self," which has been formed through the process of growing up within our unique environment and under the influence of the qualities of our community. Through the awakened, individualized will, we are able to begin to transform this everyday self—the self that is full of thinking, feeling, and will impulses belonging to what we have gained from being citizens of our surrounding sensory world. In order to carry out this transformation, we are required to differentiate the *nature* of the capacity for thinking from the *nurture* or *content* of our thoughts. The capacity to think, the capacity to feel, and the capacity to will—when liberated from the *content* of material thinking, material feeling, and material will impulses—can become a "body" equipped with the organs necessary for the perception of the *spiritual* environment all around it.

> We will find our way into the spiritual world if we follow this path and develop the forces of thinking, feeling, and willing that are usually dormant within us. We must not start with the body, as ancient Eastern cultures did, and try to control our breathing. Instead, we have to guide our development through our soul and spirit.[49]

Just as the life processes allow us to "take in" the earthly environment—enabling it to flow from the outer sensory world to the inner, everyday world of thinking, feeling, and willing—so can the spiritual body, formed out of the capacities of thinking, feeling, and willing, "take in" the content of the spiritual world around it. Once these capacities are emptied of the content gained primarily from our earthly experiences, they can be "turned" or reoriented in order to receive the spiritual content that continually emanates toward the human being from all things.

> A special disposition of soul is necessary for the acquisition of spiritual knowledge, one to which the usual disposition in everyday life on the earthly plane is radically opposed. In external life, especially in our present day, the soul is in a continual state of unrest. Throughout the day, the soul is constantly exposed to new impressions; and since it identifies itself with the impressions, it lives in a state of continuous restlessness.[50]

Our Individual Task toward Spirit-led Community

Building the "spiritual body" occurs in stages. The first step is that, out of the forces of the higher "I"—not from the everyday, restless self, but from the will activity of the higher "I"—we enter into relationship with the "other." This "other" could either be the outer world, perceptible to my senses—or my inner world, perceptible only through the ability of my "I" to look upon it in the same objective manner as we may observe the outer sensory world.

When my individualized, spiritual will is engaged in the activity of my own thinking capacity, then not only can new thoughts arise, but I am also able to observe my thinking in the same way as I look at an object outside of me. This engagement of the forces of the individualized, spiritual will can also be applied to the life of feeling; observing or witnessing my own feeling life awakens in me a greater feeling of freedom. Through this pathway, we can begin to recognize the potential for liberation from the bonds of our everyday self.

> The whole nature of the human being must be used wisely by the one who desires to enter the way. Each human being is to themselves absolutely the way, the truth, and the life. But they are only so when they grasp their whole individuality firmly, and, by the force of their awakened spiritual will, recognize this individuality not as themselves, but as that thing which they have with pain created for their own use, and by means of which they aim, as their growth slowly develops their intelligence, to reach to the life beyond individuality. When they know that for this their wonderful, complex, separated life exists, then, indeed, and then only, they are upon the way.[51]

Through this relationship of the individual will activity of the higher "I" to the "other," new thoughts arise. Others may have thought these new thoughts many times before, but they are now being thought anew by the awakened relationship between the present and active higher "I" and the "other." The capacity for new thoughts is the beginning of a process of enlivening our dead, intellectual thoughts and our capacity for purely abstract thinking. Applying our individual will to our thinking is necessary in order for this to take place. Even though in our age this may be a reasonably common experience, its importance often goes unnoticed, and it is therefore insufficiently attended to.

Those who do recognize the capacity for new thoughts also realize that these thoughts have a different quality from the thoughts of everyday thinking. If we attend to this kind of thinking, it will lead us to experience the living nature of these new thoughts. This can then open us up not only to the occasional new thought lighting up our consciousness in rare moments, but also to a state of living thinking, which can become a new capacity that is consistently accessible to us.

It is these new thoughts—these living thoughts, developed out of the relationship of the "I" to the other—that initiate the formation of the spiritually perceptive organs. This is not unlike the gestation period before the human being's birth into the sensory world, during which is formed the vehicle that enables perception and life in this

Our Individual Task toward Spirit-led Community

world—the vehicle that enables us to have individual consciousness and individual life in the earthly world.

The vehicle for spiritual participation—"a new individualized consciousness body" and "a new individualized life body"—allows for individualized participation in the spiritual world. However, this new vehicle must be developed by us, and we may do so only through our own effort in transforming those contents of the soul that are permeated with earthly thoughts and habits from the everyday self, the "me-self."

The thoughts that you think, or have thought, by means of applying individual, spiritual will to the thinking capacity—these thoughts are only alive in the present moment. It is as though they are being thought for the first time each time they are thought—even if you, or someone else, have already thought them a hundred times before. They cannot simply be "retrieved" from memory, but must be thought and experienced anew every time.

It is not everyday thinking, but *living thinking* that is developed through this engagement of the individualized will within the world of thoughts. This process plants the seed that develops toward what Rudolf Steiner termed a true *Imaginative* thinking capacity. Imaginative thinking occurs through the ensoulment—or the formation of a "skin" by the activity of the higher "I"—around four of our life processes simultaneously, thus enabling these life processes to act as one. It is the ensoulment of the four life processes of *individualizing, practicing, growing,* and *creating* that allows us to develop *Imaginative consciousness*.

Imagination, or Imaginative consciousness, is the first true spiritually perceptive capacity within the spiritual world. Although it requires the work of the awakened higher "I" activity, every individual in our time can awaken consciously the beginnings of this new capacity. Like the higher "I" development, it has been a capacity available to many—not only to a few—since the beginning of the twentieth century.

Imaginative consciousness gives us the capacity to see and perceive images that arise out of the realm of spiritual consciousness, which has a different relationship to time and space than everyday consciousness does. One step in Imaginative consciousness allows us to "foresee" the quality of the inner consequences of the various paths that we may have an opportunity to take in a given life situation. The initial experience of this foresight is to recognize which of our two selves will be strengthened by the paths lying ahead of us. Even though we will have this capacity for "pre-sight," we will still be free to choose which self we want to increase, and which self we want to decrease. We are never commanded or forbidden to take either path, for that is a matter of our individual freedom, and the choice is made in each individual heart.

When we commonly think of Imaginative thinking, we often think that it means some kind of visualizing, fantasizing, or even everyday imagination—but these are quite different from the genuine, spiritual Imaginative consciousness that is developed over time through our own effort. A clear distinction between these two can be made

Our Individual Task toward Spirit-led Community

by considering that with the everyday capacity for imagination we tend to conjure thoughts or ideas that have little to do with the reality of what surrounds us. For example, you can say to a child, "Catch this ball as if you are catching the sun." This is an example of using everyday imagination; but this is in no way the same as the Imaginative consciousness spoken of here. Such everyday imaginations do not have to do with realities. However, through true spiritual Imaginations, the "pictures" always have a genuine relationship to the surrounding spiritual world. Still, such pictures or insights may only be partial realities and therefore not yet clear Imaginations. It takes time to develop an Imaginative consciousness that is dependable and clear. However, the "foreseeing" is much easier to distinguish, as its results can be gauged within one's own inner life. Foreseeing is the first dependable step in Imaginative consciousness and it becomes a language for our individual internal guidance.

Our next stage of development as human beings is that of moving from the awakened "I" to spiritual Imaginative consciousness. We ourselves need to walk this path and we alone can achieve this development. However, there are schooling exercises that serve to train and support us on the way. They were once given in the various esoteric schools only to the chosen few, or by certain teachers to the disciples who were recognized to be fit and able to take these future steps. But because the future is now upon us, these schooling exercises have been made available to the whole world; anyone is free to utilize them if they choose to do so.

What is commonly referred to as the Buddhist Eightfold Path gives us not only the tools for this transformation, but also an understanding of how the "me-self" tends to grasp hold of daily life. Usurping the "me" will strengthen the higher "I"; it will also help us to develop a greater clarity of discernment between the two selves. It can even help us to recover aspects of soul that have been weakened through addiction; but its true function is the transformation of the "me" into the capacity for a spiritual consciousness body.

In the Eightfold Path, the word "right" is connected to our ability to find what is whole again. Wholeheartedly I seek the "right opinion," and not the opinion instilled in me by both a well-meaning community and a world that has lost itself in materialism. This can be a daunting idea to begin with—the idea that you yourself can find what, spiritually, is the "living" thing to say, to do, to give.

And in this activity, not only are we transforming the inner world and establishing spiritual principles within ourselves, but we are also living these newfound realities into the outer world, adding a new spiritual content into our community and into the material, physical life around us. It is through these exercises that we can come to recognize how our living thinking is brought into everyday experiences, and how our living efforts enliven the deadening habits of the "me-self" and awaken us to a fuller participation in life.

> It is the task of the spirit to permeate material life. And we will perish if this does not happen, because our cultural–spiritual life is so abstract, and our unspiritual

material life is governed by routine. For things to get better, the spirit must become so powerful that it can master matter.[52]

These exercises are not given for personal growth, but for human ennoblement; therefore, you should take time to understand and assess the exercises from each of these two perspectives. There are many books expressing the nature of the Eightfold Path from the point of view of personal growth. This must be clearly differentiated from the application of the Eightfold Path as an engagement of the higher "I" in daily life, enabling the soul to be in dialogue with the spiritual impulses that flow toward the world.

If we look at the Eightfold Path with the recognition that it serves to usurp the "me"—as well as the unconscious flowing of the "me" in daily life—then we perceive the exercises quite differently than if we were to regard them as enabling us to develop capacities in the sense of personal growth. In reality, they are meant to lay the foundations for a new education: a self-education of my inner life through the spirit.

To begin with, we work with one exercise per day, and the eighth exercise is taken up daily all throughout our practice. There are very few exercises on the inner development path whose full practice and accomplishment require interacting with other individuals or groups in the outer world. Couples or groups who wish to take on a collective practice can also utilize these exercises consciously. For example, they can be useful when, with higher intention, people who know each other take on the task of working individually toward bringing health into the relationship between them. The exercises can be especially useful for couples or groups who have found that fixed, unfree, or unconscious patterns are ruling their way of relating. However, we should take care not to evaluate, judge, or criticize anyone else's efforts. Even if a group commits to working with the Eightfold Path, the extent to which it is taken up is always a matter of each individual's free choice—and it is the responsibility of the individual alone to evaluate themselves.

In studying the Eightfold Path, it is useful to observe how the everyday self steps in to make judgments, even though it has not yet begun to practice the exercises of this path. You will begin to see the power that these daily exercises carry for self-transformation, regardless of whether you view them from the perspective of the everyday mind or the higher mind.

> In a sense, we have to rise above ourselves and accompany ourselves through life on a higher level, so to speak. This higher self must observe us in the same way that we usually study phenomena of nature or experiments. Only then will we learn to develop thoughts about something that for the last three or four centuries has largely been governed and motivated by our most personal emotions.[53]

In the very studying of the exercises, we learn much about the path; in the practicing of them, we walk the path. Then we can contribute to helping others on the way. Rudolf Steiner gave the following extracted passages, which summarize each of these eight attributes.

Our Individual Task toward Spirit-led Community

Saturday – Right Opinion

To pay attention to one's ideas.
   To think only significant thoughts. To learn little by little to separate in one's thoughts the essential from the nonessential, the eternal from the transitory, truth from mere opinion.
   In listening to the talk of one's fellow human beings, to try to become quite still inwardly, foregoing all assent, and still more all unfavorable judgments (criticism, rejection), even in one's thoughts and feelings.
   This may be called *"Right Opinion"*[54] [or *Right Understanding*].

Through the practice of *right opinion*, we take our self-education in hand. This practice asks us to pay attention to how our ideas are conceived. For the most part, our inner life of thought is a mishmash of associations. Usually we allow thoughts to jump, or leapfrog, one upon the other, while having only the slightest connection to one another—or, we unconsciously flare up with ideas derived from our environment. Right opinion wants to break apart the usual disjointed medley of ideas. It wants us to entertain only deep conceptions and to have them gather strength through concentration. It wants us to control our thinking by only conceiving what we choose to be attentive to, and to discriminate between significant and insignificant ideas. No longer should thought flit about, but now it should run in strong channels, self-conceived. Our thoughts achieve significance by teaching us about the world around us. Thinking should have the goal of making the world clearer and bringing it closer to us—not of alienating us with a form of thinking focused on pleasure and antipathy. Thinking should become a teacher about the world and should veer away from leading us to merely enjoy or avoid things. We attain new knowledge of the world when that knowledge is not acquired by our preferences, our likes and dislikes.

We pay attention to what presents itself to our capacity for new learning. We discover that the schooling of our life is awakening us from our particular slumber. People usually allow themselves to regard what they encounter in the course of their daily lives and earthly biographies as being formed by chance alone. We now give a new significance to this "outer" schooling, as though it were consciously instructing us. This will awaken in us an ability to discern what is transient and requiring less consideration, in contrast to what is eternal and significant. Slowly, the student pays more and more attention to the significant aspects of life. As a result of our becoming less attached to the superficial, these superficial aspects fade in significance and lose their hold on our inner lives.

Sunday – Right Judgment

> To determine on even the most insignificant matter only after fully reasoned *deliberation*. All unthinking behavior, all meaningless actions, should be kept far away from the soul. One should always have well-weighed reasons for everything. And one should definitely abstain from doing anything for which there is no significant reason.

> Once one is convinced of the rightness of a decision, one must hold fast to it, with inner steadfastness.
>
> This may be called "*Right Judgment*," having been formed independently of sympathies and antipathies.

The practice of *right judgment* wants us to pay attention to what drives our actions—and not to resolve upon a course of action without full deliberation. All meaningless action, or action based on momentary concerns, is to be kept far away from us. Right judgment asks us to establish ourselves as the strong decider of our own action, and not to be carried along unconsciously by circumstance. The usual, habitual action triggered by environmental stimuli must be replaced by action based on thoughtful consideration. The goal is to have life flow forth from an inner source and not to let it be dictated by outer circumstances. Meaningless actions are alien to the spirit within, but all actions arising from the spirit—regardless of how apparently insignificant—have a purpose. The impulses for action arising within us may stream from unknown sources; the student endeavors to recognize the source, and in doing so they become aware of certain karmic patterns that can be overcome by acting purely "in the now," according to the true, harmonious, and good that awakens in relationship to the present. By trying not to be swayed by any influences other than that of our own individual resolve, we become more conscious of the nature and experience of the "external" influences that tend to arise within us.

Monday – Right Word

> *Talking.* Only what has sense and meaning should come from the lips of one striving for higher development. All talking for the sake of talking—to kill time—is in this sense harmful.
>
> The usual kind of conversation, a disjointed medley of remarks, should be avoided. This does not mean shutting oneself off from intercourse with one's fellow human beings; it is precisely then that talk should gradually be led to significance. One adopts a thoughtful attitude to every speech and answer, taking all aspects into account. Never talk without cause—be gladly silent. One tries not to talk too much or too little. First listen quietly; then reflect on what has been said.
>
> This exercise may be called *"Right Word."*

The practice of *right word* wants us to give true expression to what we desire to communicate to the world. The normal conversation that unconsciously jumps from topic to topic must be avoided, and we must strive to bring a greater meaningfulness to our speech. The significance that we have given our thoughts through the practice of right opinion may now find an outlet to flow into the world through the practice of right word.

The student should utter no word that is without sense and meaning for the spirit; all such chatter is to be avoided. Therefore, it becomes clear that we must avoid the usual kind of conversations. This can be difficult, as some relationships are formed and maintained through the random discussion of indiscriminately varied topics. However, this does not mean that such a relationship must be lost. It is precisely here, in the old ways of talking, that the new can be observed and brought in with greater clarity—and those conversations and relationships can thereby develop a greater significance. Opportunities to converse in a meaningful way are looked for in all interactions with others. This practice not only generates awareness for ourselves, but it also opens a space for the other to step into new ways of expressing themselves with meaning and depth.

Tuesday – Right Deed

> *External actions.* These should not be disturbing for our fellow human beings. Where an occasion calls for action out of one's inner being, deliberate carefully how one can best meet the occasion—for the good of the whole, the lasting happiness of human beings, the eternal.
>
> Where one does things of one's own accord, out of one's own initiative, consider most thoroughly beforehand the effect of one's actions.
>
> This is called "*Right Deed.*"

The practice of *right deed* wants us to harmonize our actions with those of our fellow human beings and with the events in our environment. Deeds that bring us into discord with another person will have to be answered for in terms of bringing our karma into balance. We, as beings involved in the evolution of the world and the cosmos, are called to deeds that fit in with this evolution—not to deeds that hinder or distort it. Right deed also calls upon us to overcome our habitual tendency to do what pleases us or to escape what we dislike. We need to overcome our usual, routine, egocentric way of acting, and instead come at things in a fresh and new way—a way that is centered on the world in which we are placing our deeds. We need to overcome our unconscious tendencies, even when they arises from the right motives; we also need to consider how best to act or respond in such a way that we do not needlessly produce unharmonious reactions in the other. Harmonious actions have a definite effect in service of the other, and even in service of the surrounding forces.

Wednesday – Right Standpoint

> *The ordering of life.* To live in accordance with nature and spirit. Not to be swamped by the external trivialities of life. To avoid all that brings unrest and haste into life. To hurry over nothing, but also not to be indolent. To look on life as a means for working toward higher development and to behave accordingly.
> One speaks in this connection of *"Right Standpoint."*

The practice of *right standpoint* aims at the management of the whole of life—at the goal of living in accord with both nature and spirit. In this way, we strive to find the right rhythm in life, the "golden mean" between haste and laziness. We are here to work and offer up our endeavors toward a goal that is truly human. We are here not to be dissatisfied with the tasks entrusted to us, but to see them as an opportunity to bring to expression deeper and truer aspects of our spirit. We are asked to take a position in life that corresponds with the whole of the cosmos, with both nature and spirit.

We begin to perceive that our station and task in life is the very place in which we can practice our process of liberation. We do not think, "I could be freer if only I had different work or better outer circumstances"—but rather, "My livelihood is achieved through the right relationship to any 'occupation.'" Whoever finds no satisfaction in the situation in which they are placed will not be able to derive from that situation the power to unfold *right activity* in the world. And so we may recognize: through the inner activity achieved by means of living in the right way in any occupation, I can awaken the path that will lead me to the task in which my next step of liberation is to be found. If I am engaged in my work with right activity, then the present situation either deepens or comes to an end—but if I avoid applying right activity in my present situation, I also avoid developing the next step that leads me onward. In deep conversation with what is expressing itself in outer life, I look to improve myself by means of the task that I am engaged in right now.

Thursday – Right Habit

> *Human Endeavor.* One should take care to do nothing that lies beyond one's powers—but also to leave nothing undone that lies within them. To look beyond the everyday, the momentary, and to set oneself aims and ideals connected with the highest duties of a human being. For instance, in the sense of the prescribed exercises, to try to develop oneself so that afterwards one may be able all the more to help and advise one's fellow human beings—though perhaps not in the immediate future. This can be summed up as, "*To let all the foregoing exercises become a habit.*"

The practice of *right habit* asks us to change the place from which our habits usually spring. Instead of our habits coming from the unconscious aspects of our soul life, right habit wants the light of self-knowledge and the highest aspects of the human spirit to conceive our endeavors. This change toward spirit-filled endeavors allows us to set aims that have to do with the ideals and the great duties of the human being. For example: not reaching beyond what we can accomplish, yet leaving nothing undone that remains within our capabilities. Habits, as we know, are instilled in us from many varying layers or phases of our development. The student overcomes habits that do not belong to the spirit within—that do not belong to the spirit that stands in harmonious relationship to life. Because of our inscribed habits, we often unconsciously omit new possibilities that lie within our scope of achievement but for which we do not yet possess the habit. And in addition, we generally have many habits that diminish our connection to higher impulses. With the practice of right habit, we try not to become stagnant in a pattern, but instead to walk the path of self-perfecting over a long period of time.

Friday – Right Memory

The endeavor to *learn as much as possible from life.*

Nothing goes by us without giving us a chance to gain experiences that are useful for life. If one has done something wrongly or imperfectly, that becomes a motive for doing it rightly or more perfectly later on.

If one sees others doing something, one observes them with the like end in view (yet not coldly or heartlessly). And one does nothing without looking back to past experiences, which can be of assistance in one's decisions and achievements.

One can learn from everyone—even from children, if one is attentive.

This exercise is called *"Right Memory"* (remembering what has been learned from experiences).

The practice of *right memory* deals with the effort to learn as much as possible from life. We are accustomed to let life slip by as a series of bare images. We must instead instill in ourselves an energy that gathers as much learning from life as possible. We need to gather a rich store of experience that we can return to for guidance. In order to instill in ourselves this new vigor, we need to overcome our usual careless approach to life. What matters is the will to learn as much as we can from circumstances and from people. There is a need to find a balance between simply watching with an aloof attitude and studying with a warm, open interest—to form our approach in a way that is not overly sympathetic and also not with coldness. We can use our normal experiences in life as an opportunity to learn with an open heart. In this way, we also cultivate faith in the learning processes of others. Mistakes are bound to happen; it is the gesture of right memory that prevents us from repeating the same mistake over and over again. We do not detach ourselves from the human condition, but embrace it wholeheartedly with the intention of learning as much as possible.

Summary, or Right Contemplation

> To turn one's gaze inward from time to time, even if only for five minutes daily at the same time. In doing so one should sink down into oneself, carefully take counsel with oneself, test and form one's principles of life, run through in thought one's knowledge—or lack of it—weigh up one's duties, think over the contents and true purpose of life, feel genuinely pained by one's own errors and imperfections. In a word: labor to discover the essential, the enduring, and earnestly aim at goals in accord with it—for instance, virtues to be acquired. (Not to fall into the mistake of thinking that one has done something well, but to strive ever further toward the highest standards.)
>
> This exercise is called *"Right Examination"* [*Right Contemplation*].

The review of the day exercise, which involves looking back through the events of our day in reverse order, is one way that we can practice *right contemplation*. We can also do this by turning our gaze inward for five minutes daily. In this way, we sink back into our deeper inner connection and, in introspection, we form and test the fundamental principles of our life, review in thought our knowledge or lack of knowledge, weigh our duties, and reflect upon the content and aim of life. With pure devotion to the things of the world, we are to immerse ourselves in them and let them alone speak to us. We seek to find and test our underlying life intentions. What is our aim in living? What do we hope to place upon the altar of humanity? This is an opportunity to discover what is enduring and essential in life—to separate out from the daily "to and fro" what is vitally important and fundamental to life. We are to see our errors and imperfections, to be genuinely pained by them, and to aim at overcoming them. The right contemplation of life is an essential exercise to refresh and crystallize the overarching, guiding principles of our life.

Along the Eightfold Path, we must acquire right contemplation in our daily lives. This eighth quality is acquired when the student can surrender, with pure devotion, to the things of the world—thereby allowing them to speak anew. This new self-education becomes right contemplation.

All education that leads us beyond learning processes based on childhood capacities requires that the individual, awakened "I" enters into relationship with the world around it. On the basis of this relationship, all things begin to become "new." We can indeed form an inner life that is not conditioned by others or by an abstract view of the world—we can form an inner life that is independent of the opinions of others and that is connected to a new, self-awakened understanding of the world. In inner independence, we can rely solely upon the spirit to inform us of our evolutionary path—the unifying spirit that lives in each of us individually and yet works toward the evolution of the whole.

All education that leads us away from the learning acquired through "I"-activity is for personal development and the personal acquisition of knowledge. In such learning activity, we are therefore faced with resistance to the necessary extinguishing of our desires for personal gain. If we are consistently willing to overcome these personal desires, then we are ready for the "middle path" toward the spirit. On this path, we recognize that the spirit lives within us, but we also recognize that *we* can live within *it*. This leads us to a series of inner trials.

The trials are numerous, but our process of undergoing them gives rise to two distinct tendencies that we must become aware of. The first is that through these trials, we are awakened to the greater dimension of the egotism living within us—egotism that is stirred to life as a result of our own realization that the spirit lives in us. At the same time, we also become aware of the second tendency: namely, that we feel we could lose our own self in the void of a vast, undifferentiated spiritual existence.

When we live our lives "full of" our everyday self, we avoid a conscious encounter with this void. Our horror of the void is warranted, as is our concern about falling prey to an amplified spiritual egotism and pride. We must face this polarity of *extinction of the self* and *spiritual egotism*. Although there are many trials, these two diversions serve as a sort of archetype for the two poles of temptation inherent in all other trials.

In each trial, the individual becomes aware of the potential of falling into both directions of error. The shame that arises from experiencing our greater-than-imagined egoistic self, as well as our immense fear of the void—of the state of "no self"—remind us of the two chasms that dwell at each side of the middle way. The Eightfold Path seeks to help us steer through this middle way by supporting us in the practice of overcoming ourselves while at the same

Our Individual Task toward Spirit-led Community

time engaging in a differentiated spiritual life requiring our higher "I" activity.

Personal development and personal acquisition of any kind of earthly knowledge is enhanced by utilizing the life processes consciously. However, the life processes that are taken hold of by the higher "I" also serve to develop capacities for spiritual insight—capacities through which each individual may attain insight according to their soul capacities and tasks. These capacities become the strengths of that individual—strengths bestowed by a living connection with the spirit.

All learning that requires the activity of the "I" leads us to a higher life and leads the world toward healthy progress.

> All that the human "I" brings to development within will grow into love.[55]

In spiritual inner development, the life processes are worked with in a different way than they are when we use them to acquire knowledge in the sensory world. But it is nevertheless the healthy, conscious "ground of learning" established by the functioning of the seven life processes in the sensory world—developed in the course of independent learning, usually during childhood—that gives rise to these new capacities within the human being as an adult. We cannot skip over the foundations. If they have not been developed in childhood, then extra effort and care will be needed in order to form these capacities later in life. However, as we will then have outgrown the malleable developmental stage of our younger years, we will in such cases have to form them with intense soul strength that can only be gained through rigorous inner work.

It is possible that each time we engage in living activity—activity toward spiritual insight—we will experience a new thought or gain a new understanding that can illuminate life for us. However, these various insights need to be linked to each other by means of our own efforts. We no longer have the perspective ingrained in us by virtue of the fact that we normally look at the world solely from out of our "physical home"—that we look at the world through the window of our physical senses, which in itself creates a certain default point of view. We need a new "soul home," a place from which we can depart and to which we can return in our process of spiritual inquiry. Lacking this, we will be unable to build a "body" of knowledge, but rather it will seem as though we can gain only random, disconnected tidbits of insight. It must be understood that tidbits should not be shared with the world. Only Imaginations that can be communicated with full clarity are ready to be shared with others. Individuals who do not know the meaning of the insights they receive are also not ready to share them; the meaning will grow if the insight can be led toward a central point of inquiry in a scientific manner.

Applying our individualized will to our activity of thinking about our task may be enough to catalyze the process of awakening spiritual thoughts. This is a prerequisite for spiritual science.

> Spiritual science tries to push the will into our thinking, and at the same time it also trains spiritual researchers to be as objective toward the results of their own willing—that is, their actions—as they usually are only in regard to outer events.[56]

All that we investigate through our soul tasks and capacities must come together in order to form a central "body" of wisdom. In some occult schools, this is called the "building of the hut." No insight or revelation is of value in itself unless it can be tied back to a central hub of inquiry. For some, one's earthly task may be the starting point of building this "hut" or hub of soul inquiry.

The true task of the school teacher who is inquiring spiritually into a pedagogical question will lead them to a situation in which all of their insights become connected to, and useful for, the task of pedagogy. To begin with, this may be primarily for themselves as an individual teacher, and in relation to their individual work. As this body of wisdom develops, one begins to recognize that it can also be useful for all others who are in need of insight into that task.

> Once teachers and educators have taken up spiritual science, they will no longer adhere to an approach based on standards and abstract principles derived from intellectualism, telling them how they must teach. No, teachers who have undergone training in spiritual science see each child as new and unique, just as an artist views each of his or her creations as new and unrepeatable. In spiritual science, there are no abstract, didactic principles; instead, the teachers empathize with the child, and their approach is based on the child's inner being.[57]

For a health practitioner who has a spiritual insight through their living thinking, this insight will lead them to illuminate health and healing for their own work, and eventually they will be able to convey this illumination to others, thereby making it useful for the tasks of others as well. An adult teacher of inner development leads all of their insights back to the same "hub." All spiritual learning experiences inform the one undergoing them about how to work more effectively in their earthly task, both for themselves and for others—even if the other has a different task or works in a different field. Even if the various insights have opposing points of view, the task, the "hub," still unites these insights into a cohesive whole.

In this way, spiritual science overcomes the separateness of the various vocations and unites them in the spiritual wisdom of the joint task. It becomes apparent that all who are working for the science of the spirit are fundamentally working for the evolution of human consciousness on the path toward freedom and love—even though they may present opposing points of view on various matters.

We may not initially recognize it, but our "spiritual place," or vocation, is connected to our task for the community. In earthly life, some individuals are very clear about their work; they know well the task that is theirs. They have found their vocation. Whereas others find themselves doing all sorts of jobs, but not really feeling that they have found their work: the place where they can be deeply giving of their spiritual inner life and yet continually learning at the same time.

Our Individual Task toward Spirit-led Community

When it comes to working with the spirit, everyone has a task. A person's task is the area in which they give and learn in the direction of progressive spiritual unfolding—regardless of whether or not this is acknowledged as "work" (paid or otherwise) in the context of everyday life.

> Every single human being is a channel through which a spiritual world pours forth.[58]

What we learn from the spiritual world, what speaks to us, what we take in and what we give out into the physical world, what inspires us in the light of spiritual life—all of this comprises the domain of our task for our larger community. It may or may not take the form of official work within the community, but it is nonetheless our way of bringing the spirit into the world. Working in this way gives true value and meaning to our place within the community.

Far too many individuals are absorbed in jobs that constitute a paid livelihood, but that deprive them of being able to engage themselves fully. They do not feel themselves to be in the right place, in the right mode of service. We do a disservice to individuals when we fail, as a community, to look upon our fellow community members with the aim of helping the right person to be in the right place or position. We would do an even greater disservice if we were to replace an individual's opportunity to carry out their tasks—for example, if we were to take the task away as a result of the opinion that artificial intelligence can be more productive than a human being.

> If life continues without the stimuli that come from the spiritual world, industry can go on, banks can continue to exist, as well as universities where all the sciences are taught, other professions can be developed—but everything will lead to decadence, to barbarism, to the fall of civilization.[59]

We can understand our soul task by looking at how we already experience the new thoughts working in us. How does the spirit speak within you—what new content seems to stream to you? You can ask yourself: What inwardly speaks to me? What enlivens me, from out of the spirit, in what has already been conveyed by others? When reflecting on a book you have read, or a lecture you have heard, containing spiritual content, what aspects do you take in and what aspects live on in you? What continues to resonate and resound after you've laid down that book or left that lecture? You may find, when surveying your path, that there is a consistent theme in terms of what lights up within your own being. You can also reflect on the question: Where do the creative forces work through me? Where do I feel I have created something new from out of my own liberated inner life that can be worked into the world, even in the smallest of ways?

> The human being must become a partaker of the spirit in order to carry its revelations into the physical world. We transform the earth by implanting in it what we have ascertained in the spiritual world. That is our task. It is

only because the physical world is dependent upon the spiritual, and because the human being can work upon earth in a true sense only if they are a participator in those worlds in which the creative forces lie concealed—only for these reasons should one have the desire to ascend to the higher worlds.[60]

Once we have an understanding of how our capacities are being utilized, we can increase our attentiveness in a directed way and more clearly approach the work of building a body of spiritual knowledge. Although all insights or revelations are strengthening to us, if they do not connect to where we are engaged in daily life then they become less useful in terms of how we can live with them. What we recognize as our capacities are developed further through our ability to give to the world; our capacities are then practiced through living the insights. When a person lacks a means of expressing their insights, this may induce a sort of inner "split"—a condition in which the spiritual insights can only be retained in thought but cannot be transformed into the sphere of life.

When in courts of law the deeds of human beings are viewed with the eyes of spiritual perception, when at the bed of the sick the doctor spiritually perceives and heals with spiritual insight, when in the schools the teacher works with the growing child on the basis of spiritual knowledge, when in the very streets people think and feel and act spiritually, then we shall have reached our ideal, for spiritual science will have become common knowledge.[61]

In transforming community, it is essential that your own direct insights are lived by you into life; and the more they can affect your way of living together with others, the more useful they are. It is extremely important, as the forces of physical decline enter our lives in our late thirties, that we do not allow these forces to take our inner world into death processes also. In fact, the deteriorating physical forces are just another opportunity to liberate our soul forces. This choice, which is given to every individual destiny on a microcosmic level, is an event that is now also taking place macrocosmically among the collective whole of humanity, as humanity as a whole enters more and more into physical decline. The personal decision regarding which path we will choose to unite ourselves with is still required, but the collective results of these individual decisions are now urgently weighing upon us. As our individual physical body deteriorates, will our soul life bind more and more to materialism—or will our soul life rise, transformed, through the decline of the physical body?

> Spiritual researchers who, at the age of forty, stop cultivating a continuous lively relationship to the knowledge to be gained will starve from a lack of soul–spiritual content, just as we would starve if we stopped eating at age forty. Abstract knowledge, which has gained so much ground because of the natural sciences, is satisfied with mere phenomena; it leads to once and for all, final conclusions. Spiritual knowledge, on the other hand, brings us into a living relationship to our surroundings; it must be continuously renewed if it is not to wither and die. Spiritual knowledge functions on a higher level of our life, as food does on a lower one.[62]

Our Individual Task toward Spirit-led Community

Some individuals recognize that they are fortunate because they have a worldly task that is united with their spiritual task. Through this worldly task, all of their spiritual insights are led back toward the aim of transforming the world. They have a living experience in which the spiritual world, working through their individuality, is able to transform earthly life. Through working with others who are also working in this way, community life is gradually transformed.

When as few as seven individuals who share this approach to their inner tasks come together consciously, in connection with each other, and within an outer community structure—for example, as teachers in a school community, as members of a farming community, or as a community of health practitioners working together—then this small group may open a portal to progressive spiritual forces of a higher order, calling upon them to influence the life sphere of that community.

In the effort to build community from above down, it is also necessary for some that we develop community that is not exclusively locally based. Therefore, individuals who do not work in the same physical community, but who do work together consciously with the aim of carrying a particular field of work into various outer communities, can renew the spiritual forces flowing into their common task through this method of staying connected with each other.

Seven is the number of the principle of life—the realm in which community takes root. Seven individuals, when united in this way, can begin to change the spiritual impulses working behind the existing community forms. From the heights of our circle of togetherness in the spiritual world all the way down to our diverse, particular tasks in the life of humanity, we may work hand in hand with our colleagues who are committed to this common task—who are committed to the spirit, which needs this collective working together in order to assist us in community change.

> Whether I can help, I know not; an individual helps not, but those who combine themselves with many at the proper hour. We will postpone the evil, and keep hoping. Hold thy circle fast....
> We are assembled at the propitious hour; let each perform their task; let each do their duty; and a universal happiness will swallow up our individual sorrows, as a universal grief consumes our individual joys.[63]

☙

As has been described in more detail above, the four life processes of *individualizing, practicing, growing,* and *creating*—ensouled by the active higher "I"—become the vessel by means of which each individual may receive spiritual Imaginations. This is a step beyond the capacity for living thinking. The "Imagination body" allows us to become conscious of other ways of receiving knowledge and wisdom. No other kind of earthly thinking can become an organ of perception for the spiritual world's wisdom, an organ for perceiving the spiritual world's thoughts.

> I want to know how God created this world. I am not interested in this or that phenomenon, in the spectrum

of this or that element. I want to know His thoughts, the rest are details. (Albert Einstein)[64]

We should not assume that these spiritual Imaginations have nothing to do with our outer life; in fact, they have everything to do with human life and evolution. Imaginative thinking allows us to perceive not only the spiritual thoughts in the spiritual world, but *the spiritual within the earthly world*. What lies concealed from our everyday self awakens for us through this newfound capacity. Spiritual perception of the spirit in the earthly world is a necessity in our evolution.

We, as a collective humanity, are offered numerous paths on which to step forward into the future. Only a foreseeing can know the outcome of these various paths. We are not commanded to walk the path that serves the care and development of the world. And if we have the ability to foresee, this only means that our choice becomes a conscious one. We shall decide which part of our being will lead the way. The higher "I" and the everyday self cannot rule simultaneously; one must be in abeyance. It is up to each of us at this stage of evolution to determine which self will lead the way every time a choice stands before us. This happens in small and large ways numerous times each day. Some choices have a far greater impact than others on our destiny as individuals and as a community. Without this foreseeing capacity, we may easily overlook the weight of the importance of these choices. This foreseeing capacity, available to us through Imaginative consciousness, awakens us to the impact of the potential results inherent in the possibilities before us.

Imaginative consciousness also awakens us to the reality that everything we see in the surrounding natural sensory world, including of course our own bodies, has a spiritual counterpart. Behind or within the appearance of every created thing, there lives a spiritual thought and a consciousness. Every manifest kingdom of the natural world has a spiritual consciousness as an essential part of it. We cannot consider these consciousnesses to be moral or immoral; we can only regard them as spirit-created, sense-perceptible kingdoms. It is in this sense that we feel more connected and harmonious after allowing these spirit kingdoms of nature to impress upon the spirit kingdom in us.

The natural world around us is a form of nourishment for the deeper aspects of the human being. And, likewise, we would be unable to sustain ourselves on a purely material level without our relationship to these kingdoms. But more is given to us through the kingdoms of nature than our delight in what they bring to our feeling life. And more is given to us than nourishment for the physical body. Everything in the universe that is born into the sensory world has a consciousness behind it. The manifestation of the natural world is the manifestation of the spiritual world; the spiritual consciousness behind a given thing or being is what serves the deeper aspects of the human being.

Many are able to recognize this health-giving relationship that human beings have with the natural world. We can experience it when taking a long walk in nature and allowing it to have an effect upon us—not while being full of our everyday selves, but while being inwardly present to the kingdoms that surround us. This allows us to experience the spiritual nature of these kingdoms and to take this spiritual nature into ourselves.

The balancing forces of the plant world are revealed to us every time we recognize how nature overcomes the imbalances of the materialistic world. When we come to the point of consciously recognizing the nature forces not only as material substance, but also as consciousnesses, then this serves to balance us all the more. In this way, we can perceive how humanity's inner development leads not only to health for the soul, but also to health and strength for the body. When we resolve to participate consciously with the spiritual forces, there is no hindrance that can stand in the way of the spiritual world, which reciprocally wishes to participate with us.

> The spiritual scientist takes the viewpoint that through what spiritual science brings forward about the suprasensory world—that world which we do not know with external senses, but which we must quietly call to life within us—we make our soul so active that its activity comes into harmony with that of the spiritual world, out of which our whole organism has been created.[65]

When we observe the plant kingdom, what takes place between our sensing–observation (through the twelve senses) and our inner world of development (through the interrelating of the seven life processes) is an exchange between our own consciousness and the consciousnesses of the "other." The natural, harmonious activities that have created the outer world are imbued with the same spiritual substances as we ourselves are. The expressions of the plant world, the mineral kingdom, and the animal kingdom contain these spiritual forces, and we are nourished through the interchange we have with the forces living behind these kingdoms. When we encounter them, we are "ingesting" them—not physically, but spiritually. There are certain inner exercises that require our working with nature, such as the "living and dying plant exercise."[66] In this exercise, you compare the inner experience of perceiving a living, growing, flourishing plant to that of perceiving a dying, withering plant. As one looks with the senses upon the plant, the inner activity is observed. There is a vast difference, in our inner world, between our experiences of these two conditions of the plant. However, this exercise cannot be achieved through a screen. No matter how many trees we see on a screen, we cannot receive from such experiences the necessary inner activity. We can produce a paler version of such inner activity for ourselves by summoning a memory of practicing this exercise with real trees, but we cannot newly receive this inner activity from the screen-generated image.

When the human being enters into relationship with the elements of the external sensory world, they also enter into a relationship with the consciousnesses behind the appearances. But our world is no longer purely spirit created; it has become a human-made world, born of the relationship between the spiritual world and what lives in the human being.

Try looking at a human-made object, such as a candle. The candle has been created through the activity of the human being in relationship with the spiritually born substance of the sensory world. Observe what effects this candle has on your inner being, and how the various doorways of the various senses are utilized. Now try looking at a candle on the "human-invented" computer screen and observe the difference in terms of what is fed, nourished, or activated within the soul, as well as how the various doorways of the senses are dramatically diminished.

The freedom bestowed upon our human potential means that we can utilize this world in accordance with any desire—whether greed or service, vanity or progression. What we create can feed different parts of the human being; everything we engage with feeds us in different ways according to its nature and the spiritual forces working behind it, as well as the spiritual forces working behind our own being.

We must come to recognize the various desires in ourselves and in others. Just as we "reach" toward perceiving the consciousness behind the outer appearances of things in the natural world, so we can also reach toward perceiving behind the earthly, material desires of the other's inner world. We can recognize the soul and spirit elements that are above these desires—not only in ourselves, but also in others.

> We have to deal with each other in a way that respects, protects, honors, and loves the spirit and soul in each

other; in other words, we have to go beyond what people usually believe they meet in their fellow beings.[67]

If we want to know the spiritual content behind the inner life of the other, then we must be able to extinguish the earthly, intellectual *content* of thinking so that we are left purely with our *capacity* to think. Then, the spiritual counterpart of thought content—namely, the Imaginations—can enter into relationship with our freed capacity to receive them.

If you are full of one, then you are devoid of the other. If you empty yourself of earthbound thoughts, then through the ensouled life processes you will be able to receive spiritual thoughts and Imaginations.

Spiritual *Inspiration* is developed by "putting a skin around"—or ensouling out of the higher "I"—the three other higher life processes of *perceiving*, *relating*, and *assimilating*, in such a way that they, too, may work as a unity. The higher "I" with its developed capacity for Imagination, which can perceive the spiritual pictures behind the presentations of the external world, is available to the many, not just to a few. But through this greater inner development of Inspiration, we can also awaken to experiencing the beings—the consciousnesses—that have created those spiritual Imaginations behind the external world in the first place. We will be able to read the truth and origin of the Imagination because we will know what being created it. The fullness of this capacity is still only accessible to individuals walking the path of inner development in complete consciousness.

By ensouling all seven life processes simultaneously, we develop the capacity of *Intuition*. What was once outside and what is inside are no longer divided. All that is outside is perceived as inside; I am now at one with the consciousnesses, the beings, and the creators of the perceived world.

> Human beings transform the world through their own spirit when they share their spirit with the world, by quickening their thoughts to Imagination, Inspiration, and Intuition—thus fulfilling the spiritual communion of humanity.[68]

If I come to know something through the capacity of spiritual Intuition, then what I come to know is not only my own knowledge of another being, but it is now *united with my very being*. But we ourselves must be prepared to develop the capacity to become ripe for experiencing truths in this way. Experiences of such truths are not withheld from anyone who has developed the capacity to care for them. We must never betray, misuse, or neglect such spiritual gifts.

A Vase

> I am always holding a priceless vase in my hands.
> If you asked me about the deeper truths
>   of the path and I told you
>   the answers,
> it would be like handing sacred relics to you.
> But most have their hands tied
>   behind their
>   back;

> That is, most are not free of events their eyes have seen
> and their ears have heard
> and their bodies have felt.
> Most cannot focus their abilities
> in the present, and
> might drop what
> I said.
> So I'll wait; I don't mind waiting until
> your love for all
> makes luminous
> the now. —*Rabia*[69]

The awaking to the higher "I" in the sensory world is not the same as the birth of the higher "I" in the spiritual world. In order for the higher "I" to be born in the world of spirit, the higher "I" requires a vehicle that can provide it with the necessary "skin"; this skin enables it not only to retain its individual consciousness among other consciousnesses in the vast ocean of consciousness, but to live spiritually. The birth of the higher "I" requires a "body of life." The skin developed through the cultivation of Inspiration is the beginning formation of the skin needed for the birth of the higher "I" within the spiritual world.

Just as the spirit that is being born into the sensory world requires the bodily vehicle so that it can participate fully in the world, so the spirit requires a vehicle in order to participate in the spiritual world. Imagination, Inspiration, and Intuition are the transformed thinking, feeling, and willing capacities of the higher "I" within the spiritual world. The first sheath that allows for the perception of the spiritual world out of the forces of the "I" is developed through the transformation of the personal soul. It is called *spirit self* in some Western traditions, and *Manas* in some Eastern traditions.

Without the new "body," we can know nothing of the spiritual world. I only know for sure that the spiritual world exists because the spirit in me confirms the reality of spiritual existence. But I cannot know what kind of world I exist in until I have gained the body of perception corresponding to that world. The undeveloped soul is carried into the spiritual world by the awakened "I"—but without the body capable of perceiving within that world, the soul merely finds itself in a bliss-like state that it cannot free itself from. Although a bliss-like state is often longed for within many traditions, if the experience of this state is not under the control of the individual, and if it has not been founded on a capacity for spiritual wisdom, then it indicates a premature or partial transformation of the soul.

If a child were born into the sensory world without sense organs, it would be unable to know about this world. If the soul were "reborn"—born a second time—into the spiritual world without the organs required for perceiving in that world, then it would be born ill-equipped to participate fully in that world. Not only would the soul be born unaware of itself within that world—it would also be born unaware of the other beings in that world.

All that we can utilize as a vehicle in the spiritual world is formed out of what was once a part of our everyday selves. Imaginations are living thoughts and pictures, streaming from the spiritual world into my thinking capacity and giving me new and renewed spiritual content in my thinking. These creative thoughts can bring us to direct realizations of what needs to take place in our human life in order to create community based on spirit.

Each individual who walks this path through awakening for themselves their own higher "I"—and, through the activity of the higher "I," freeing the thinking capacity from its habitual content so that it may receive spiritual content in the form of living thoughts and Imaginations—will increasingly be able to bring facets of the truth of the spiritual world into the earthly world around them.

Spiritual science—that is, living spiritual content received by individual human beings and shared with the world—also nourishes the souls of others.

> When anthroposophic content is experienced in the right frame of mind by a group of human beings whose souls wake up in the encounter with each other, the soul is lifted in reality into a spirit community.[70]

As we learn to develop a relationship with the spiritual laws that are becoming the content of our inner life through our spiritual inquiry (for example, the laws expressed in the Eightfold Path), we increasingly convey these laws into the world around us through our tasks, through our living, and through all our encounters with others.

These Imaginations and Inspirations—our transformed inner life—become as though powers of the soul that fill us with new content. However, they are only present as living spiritual consciousnesses when we are livingly present with them—which means, when we are working into

Our Individual Task toward Spirit-led Community

the world out of our awakened "I" and not out of our everyday self. They can affect our way of relating to every encounter we have in life, and their influence can illuminate the way we envision and approach our tasks in the world. But, again, they can have such an effectiveness only through the inner reality of our living presence with them. It is in this light that we can understand the esoteric statement, "An initiate is not always an initiate."

The *spirit self* opens us to perceptions and consciousness in the spiritual world, but it is not the only necessary result of our earthly vehicle's transformation. To awaken into a spiritual life in the full sense of the word, we must also be able to have a spiritual life *within the spiritual world*. This is a step in the distant future for humanity as a whole, but individuals on this path who are working into the future—the initiates—can take this step once the preparatory steps have been surmounted. This allows them to participate in the content of the spirit not only in their earthly lives, but also as citizens of the living spiritual community. This second "body" is called *life spirit* in some Western traditions, and *Buddhi* in some Eastern traditions. A beginning toward developing this *life spirit* is necessary before the birth of the higher "I" in the spiritual world can take place. If we have developed the right vehicle, then our healthy higher birth into the spiritual world is assured.

In the poem *Dark Night of the Soul* by Saint John of the Cross, we are given a beautiful expression of the individual's experience of the birth of this higher "I." This poem—although expressed through the eye of the mystic—contains within it genuine occult symbols that can help the individual to navigate and orient themselves in the context of these profound spiritual experiences.

Dark Night of the Soul

On a dark night,
kindled in love with yearnings—oh the sheer grace!
I went forth without being observed,
my house being now at rest.

In darkness and secure,
by the secret ladder, disguised—oh the sheer grace!
in darkness and in concealment,
my house being now at rest.

In the happy night,
in secret, when none saw me,
nor I beheld aught,
without light or guide, save that which burned in my heart.

This light guided me
more surely than the light of noonday
to the place where he (well I knew who!)
    was awaiting me—
a place where none appeared.

Oh, night that guided me,
oh, night more lovely than the dawn,
oh, night that joined Beloved with lover,
lover transformed in the Beloved!

Upon my flowery breast,
kept wholly for himself alone,
there he stayed sleeping, and I caressed him,
and the fanning of the cedars made a breeze.

Our Individual Task toward Spirit-led Community

> The breeze blew from the turret
> as I parted his locks;
> with his gentle hand he wounded my neck
> and caused all my senses to be suspended.
>
> I remained, lost in oblivion;
> my face I reclined on the Beloved.
> All ceased and I abandoned myself,
> leaving my cares forgotten among the lilies.
> – *Saint John of the Cross*[71]

Many assume that the "dark night of the soul" must be connected with human struggles and difficulties in the sensory world; the term is often used to describe a trial or great hardship. However, the expression originates with Saint John of the Cross. And, if well prepared, the "dark night of the soul" is the second birth that allows the individual to be born into new community, a community of the spirit.

Out of a deep understanding of the path toward spiritual community, we can recognize the coherence and interconnection of the wise insights that have streamed to humanity throughout the ages, and that still assist humanity precisely because they arose out of individualized spiritual experience. Insights like those of the *Dark Night of the Soul* and the Eightfold Path will continue to help humanity for centuries and for millennia after they were originally brought to expression.

> The more completely the soul begins to feel at home in the spiritual worlds, the more it feels lovelessness and the lack of fellow-feeling to be a denial of spirit itself.[72]

Walking this transformative path may well bear extraordinary results in the life of the individual soul; but in order to truly walk this initiation path, a person must be willing to lay down their personal soul-bearing life for the sake of higher development. This is why this path is so difficult, and why the dark night of the soul has come to be seen as a trial of great hardship.

Why would anyone choose to walk this difficult path of self-transformation when the self that motivates us in the earthly world—with ambition, desire, and comfort, those soul states that prevent us from rising up against the deceptions of the material gains we have grown accustomed to—does not achieve any fulfillment in the world of the spirit? The fact is that this path reduces personal power, pleasure, and gain—and the trials along the path test us to make sure that we are freely willing to surrender them all.

What you seek is also seeking you.[73]

Our development is called forth by the higher self, the spark of the divine spirit in each one of us—the divine spirit that is love. It is the spark of love that calls individuals forward. It is love for the other that prepares individuals to lay aside their impulses to strive for personal gain. How vast, then, must be the love summoned by the great spiritual teachers, the great initiates—those who have devoted their entire lives to the advancement of the spirit in humanity.

All who are drawn to this path know the "crack in the armor of their egoism" that allows the divine spirit to shine through: the spirit that we follow onward. We come to know for ourselves that the divine spirit is love. No degree of self-love or self-esteem—however great—is strong enough to awaken our will to walk continuously on this transformative path.

> When it is said that the soul needs preparation before it is able to have experiences in the suprasensory world, it should be added that one of the many means of preparation is the capacity for true love.[74]

At some point on the path of initiation, we awaken to its essential message: the whole path we have been walking upon is a training, and this training has prepared us for true love. We truly know this for ourselves only in those places in our soul where we are free. We can come to the recognition that without change in the direction of the spirit, we are not going to fulfill our destiny as humanity. We do not need more war in order to create this change; we need to proceed further toward love.

We now become aware that, in fact, all spiritual awakening is about love, and all awakenings that do not partake in love are not ultimately a part of this truly human future.

> Only inasmuch as love arises in humankind is true creative work being done for the cosmic future.[75]

Awaking to the "I" is the beginning of the journey of love. Although this awakening begins, as already described, in seed form—which we can awaken to and become aware of in the world of the senses—it grows beyond the seed form through the inner transformative path, eventually becoming an experience of a new being, a being of love.

This eternal self does not reside in the sensory world, but in the spiritual world—the spiritual world that it never fully leaves. A spirit that is pure divine consciousness *is* love.

In this spiritual world of love, we will also gain strengths through the "vehicle" that creates for us our basic point of view, in accordance with the soul capacities we have developed and the tasks we have taken on. Our strengths are various aspects of this love or divine consciousness.

Through building the "spiritual hut"—which requires us to relate all of our findings back to a central "place" in which we can slowly build a body of knowledge over time—we can grow that capacity to love and share it with others through all our relationships.

> True love is rooted in the spirit. Only when an individual finds their fellow human beings in the spirit do they find them with indissoluble, unswerving love.[76]

This can mean that, in the beginning, we may receive only one facet of the full reality of love, which we can then express to the world. This single capacity can still give us the strength to feel equipped with the ability to meet the difficulties within the world. But wherever we are on the path of this great journey toward love, we must recognize that in order to grow this love into the world, we need a community. We know that we need to find friends, colleagues, and community members in order to unfold our own capacities further.

Transforming our personal soul allows us to receive these Imaginations from the spiritual hierarchy just above the human being—the hierarchy of the angels. When transforming ourselves further through our work with others, we may receive Imaginations from the hierarchy of the archangels. Rudolf Steiner presented a "Collegium Imagination" to a teaching community in order to illustrate how the workings of the spiritual hierarchies can interact with us.

This Imagination shows us the way in which the hierarchies work when they engage with all groups of people who are consciously working together in any community. These hierarchies assist those who are choosing to work together in their striving toward the spirit-led community.

This Christian terminology is used here in order to understand and clearly differentiate the workings of the spiritual consciousnesses that engage with: each human being (angel), a group of human beings (archangels), and humanity as a whole (archai). We could also use a Buddhist representation of the stages of consciousness as follows: Buddha, Bodhisattva, and Dhyani–Buddha.

On the initiation path, the terms for the three higher sheaths, developed through the transformation of the lower self, are: *spirit self*, *life spirit*, and *spirit human being*. Or: *Manas*, *Buddhi*, and *Atma*. The human being slowly develops these three higher sheaths out of themselves as they continue to evolve upon the path willed by the highest spiritual consciousnesses. These three higher sheaths correspond with the three hierarchies of beings dwelling above the human kingdom.

The Collegium Imagination is meant to be brought to life inwardly by each individual in the group. It has been presented as a spiritual Imagination by Rudolf Steiner, who himself received it directly as a real, living picture of the workings of the spiritual world. However, it lives as a spiritual reality that each individual may themselves receive directly anew. When we prepare the soul through working with a spiritually bestowed Imagination that is true to spiritual realities, we can come closer to the truth for ourselves. The words below represent the essence of the hierarchy's participation. But as it is an Imagination exercise, we should take care not to be too fixated on the words; rather, we should focus on dynamically re-creating this inner picture, which has been given to us in the form of a true Imagination of the way the hierarchies of spiritual consciousnesses work with groups of individuals.

Here is the description of the Imagination, as it was recounted by someone who was present at Rudolf Steiner's lecture:

> Imagine, how behind each of you stands your angel. The angel wishes to give strength. Circling above all of you, carrying the fruit of your work and your experiences from one to another, is a ring of archangels. From their cycling and carrying, the archangels form a vessel of courage. From the heights, the good Spirit of the Time, who is one of the archai, allows a drop of light to fall into the vessel. In this manner, the archai give a drop of light.[77]

Through this Imaginative picture, we can enter into our communal working together from above downward into the world. We see the way in which the higher spiritual forces require us to work together, as well as how the Spirit of our Time gives to those who can join in this larger task—which is likewise each of their own task. Each of us can be strengthened through our participation in a group that consciously acknowledges and works with the spiritual hierarchies.

When we read Rudolf Steiner's "fundamental social law" with this picture of the individualized strengths that arise from our working with the hierarchies, then we can see the process from another point of view: the point of view of the new community, originating from above and flowing down into a transforming of the world.

> A healthy social life is found,
> when in the mirror of each human soul
> the whole community is shaped,
> and when in the community
> lives the strength of each human soul.[78]

The strength of the individual soul is the new strength that each of us needs to meet what we must face in these important times. Not that strength which we have as an inheritance of our divine origin, but our new, living strength gained by our ever-awakening relationship to the spiritual world: a strength that can grow as we transform the everyday self. It is a strength that, when united with the strengths of others, can unite with the progressive spiritual powers that are working for our present collective human task—that of bringing humanity ever closer to becoming beings who love in freedom and through free deeds. Love and freedom are synonymous for human beings within the spiritual world; and through the development of spirit-led community, they will increasingly come to be synonymous with life on earth. Then we will recognize that the true freedom we all seek can only be a freedom united with love.

Notes

1. See Eckhart Tolle, *The Power of Now: A Guide to Spiritual Enlightenment* (Vancouver, BC: Namaste, 1999), the introduction.
2. Rudolf Steiner, *Soul Economy: Body, Soul, and Spirit in Waldorf Education*, tr. R. Everett (Great Barrington, MA: Anthroposophic Press, 2003), CW 303, lect. of Jan. 3, 1922.
3. See Michael Winnick, "Putting a Finger on Our Phone Obsession," June 16, 2016; https://blog.dscout.com/mobile-touches (accessed Nov. 27, 2017).
4. This project is known as "XPRIZE"; see: https://learning.xprize.org/about/overview (accessed Nov. 27, 2017).
5. Rudolf Steiner, *The Book of Revelation and the Work of the Priest* (Forest Row, UK: Rudolf Steiner Press, 1998), CW 346, lect. of Sept. 22, 1924, p. 254.
6. Emil Bock, *The Apocalypse of Saint John*, tr. A. Heidenreich (Edinburgh: Floris Books, 2005).
7. Rudolf Steiner, "Some Characteristics of Today," tr. H. Collison, CW 193, lect. of June 12, 1919.
8. Rudolf Steiner, *Karmic Relationships: Esoteric Studies: Esoteric Studies,* vol. 4 (Forest Row, UK: Rudolf Steiner Press, 1983), CW 238, lect. of Sept. 23, 1924.
9. Helen Dukas and Banesh Hoffmann, *Albert Einstein: The Human Side: New Glimpses from His Archives* (Princeton, NJ: Princeton University, 1979), p. 66.
10. This is a rewording of a thought by Rumi from his poem "Love Dogs": "This longing you express *is* the return message"; in *The Essential Rumi*, tr. C. Barks (New York: HarperCollins, 1995), p. 155.
11. Lisa Romero, *The Inner Work Path: A Foundation for Meditative Practice in the Light of Anthroposophy* (Great Barrington, MA: SteinerBooks, 2014).

12 Rudolf Steiner, *Knowledge of the Higher Worlds and Its Attainment*, tr. G. Metaxa and H. and L. Monges (New York: Anthroposophic Press, 1947), CW 10, chap. 1, "How Is Knowledge of the Higher Worlds Attained?" pp. 9–13, tr. adapted; other translations: *Knowledge of the Higher Worlds: How Is It Achieved?* tr. D. S. Osmond and C. Davy (Forest Row, UK: Rudolf Steiner Press, 2009); *How to Know Higher Worlds,* tr. C. Bamford (Hudson, NY: Anthroposophic Press, 1994).

13 Rudolf Steiner, *Knowledge of the Higher Worlds and Its Attainment*, p. 23, tr. adapted.

14 *Love Poems from God: Twelve Sacred Voices from the East and West,* tr. D. Ladinsky, (NY: Penguin Books, 2002), p. 224.

15 J. W. von Goethe, *Faust, Part One*, tr. D. Luke (Oxford, UK: Oxford University, 2008), lines 1,110–1,125.

16 Rudolf Steiner, *Knowledge of the Higher Worlds and Its Attainment*, p. 17.

17 Rudolf Steiner, *Awakening to Community*, tr. M. Spock (Spring Valley, NY: Anthroposophic Press, 1974), CW 257, lect. of Feb. 27, 1923.

18 Rudolf Steiner, *The Connection between the Living and the Dead*, tr. A. Jackson (Great Barrington, MA: SteinerBooks, 2017), CW 168, lect. of Oct. 10, 1916, "How Can Today's Poverty of Soul be Overcome?"

19 *Educaredo.org. EduCareDo* offers a self-directed study course based on the principal ideas of Rudolf Steiner, which he called Anthroposophy. Readings, experiments, exercises, and activities—including the basic exercises toward inner development and meditation—comprise the twenty-six lessons, which are sent fortnightly over twelve months. The course provides a sequential, clear, and practical approach to understanding and applying the principles of Anthroposophy to many disciplines in life. Health practitioners, social workers, teachers, parents, farmers, gardeners, artists, tradespeople, administrators, and scientists work with and refer back to the *EduCareDo* lessons and community for many years. *EduCareDo* functions as a growing community, in which members strive to enliven and support one another in their individual tasks. The course fees collected by *EduCareDo* are re-invested into projects around the world.

Notes

20 Dukas and Hoffmann, *Albert Einstein: The Human Side*, p. 33.

21 Ladinsky (ed.), *Love Poems from God*, p. 286.

22 Ibid., p. 312.

23 Rudolf Steiner, *Awakening to Community*, lect. of Mar. 4, 1923.

24 Ladinsky (ed.), *Love Poems from God*, p. 220.

25 Rudolf Steiner, *Macrocosm and Microcosm*, tr. D. S. Osmond and C. Davy (Forest Row, UK: Rudolf Steiner Press, 1985), CW 119, lect. of March 29, 1910, tr. adapted.

26 Rudolf Steiner, *Metamorphoses of the Soul: Paths of Experience,* vol. 1, tr. C. Davy and C. v. Arnim (Forest Row, UK: Rudolf Steiner Press, 1983), CW 58, lect. Nov. 25, 1909; revised ed., *Transforming the Soul,* vol. 1 (Forest Row, UK: Rudolf Steiner Press, 2005).

27 Rudolf Steiner, *Practical Advice to Teachers*, tr. J. Collis (Great Barrington, MA: Anthroposophic Press, 2000), CW 294, lect. Aug. 25, 1919, pp. 52–53.

28 Rudolf Steiner, *Origin and Goal of the Human Being*, CW 53, lect. Mar. 30, 1905.

29 Rudolf Steiner, ibid.

30 Justin Rosenstein, quoted in "Former Facebook investor's damning words on tech giant," Nov. 11, 2017: http://www.nzherald.co.nz/business/news/article.cfm?c_id=3&objectid=11943088 (accessed Nov. 28, 2017).

31 See: https://habitsummit.com/ (accessed Nov. 28, 2017).

32 James Williams, quoted in the article by Paul Lewis: "'Our minds can be hijacked': the tech insiders who fear a smartphone dystopia," October 6, 2017, posted at: https://www.theguardian.com/technology/2017/oct/05/smartphone-addiction-silicon-valley-dystopia (accessed Nov. 28, 2017).

33 James Williams, ibid.

34 Emil Bock, *The Apocalypse of Saint John* (op. cit.), pp. 118–119.

35 See, for example, the article by Kelly Grant, "The Pressure of Big Pharma," June 19, 2017; https://www.theglobeandmail.com/news/national/the-pressure-of-big-pharma-financial-conflicts-of-interest-common-on-medical-guidelinepanels/article35389639 (accessed Nov. 28, 2017).

36 Emil Bock, *The Apocalypse of Saint John*, p. 120.

37 Rudolf Steiner, "The Work of the Angels in the Human Astral Body," trans. D.S. Osmond and O. Barfield, CW 182, lect. of Oct. 9, 1918; also, *Death as a Metamorphosis of Life* (Great Barrington, MA: SteinerBooks, 2008).

38 Rudolf Steiner, *Our Connection with the Elemental World*, trans. S. Blaxland-de Lange (Forest Row, UK: Rudolf Steiner Press, 2016), CW 158, lect. of Apr. 11, 1912, p. 176.

39 Rudolf Steiner, *The Book of Revelation and the Work of the Priest* (op. cit.), lect. of Sept. 22, 1924, pp. 254–255.

40 This is a rewording of a thought by Rumi; see note 10.

41 Rudolf Steiner, "Education for Adolescents," lect. of June 21, 1922, CW 302a; in *The Journal for Anthroposophy*, spring 1979, tr. adapted.

42 Rudolf Steiner, ibid.

43 Rudolf Steiner, *Knowledge of Soul and Spirit*, CW 56, lect. of Mar. 12, 1908, tr. T. O'Keefe from *Die Erkenntnis der Seele und des Geistes* (Dornach, 1985), p. 252.

44 Lisa Romero, *Living Inner Development: The Necessity of True Inner Development in the Light of Anthroposophy* (Great Barrington, MA: SteinerBooks, 2016).

45 Rudolf Steiner, *Social Issues: Meditative Thinking and the Threefold Social Order* (Hudson, NY: Anthroposophic Press, 1991), CW 334, lect. Mar. 18, 1920.

46 Rudolf Steiner, *Knowledge of the Higher Worlds and Its Attainment*, p. 27.

47 Rudolf Steiner, *The Book of Revelation and the Work of the Priest* (op. cit.), lect. of Sept. 22, 1924.

48 Rudolf Steiner, *Occult Science: An Outline*, tr. G. and M. Adams (London: Rudolf Steiner Press, 1979) p. 241.

49 Rudolf Steiner, *Social Issues* (op. cit.), lect. Jan. 5, 1920.

50 Rudolf Steiner, *Life between Death and Rebirth* (Anthroposophic Press, 1968), CW 140, lect. of Oct. 26, 1912.

51 Mabel Collins, *Light on the Path* (Pasadena, CA: Theosophical University Press, 1997), part 1, no. 20, pp. 5–6; tr. adapted.

52 Rudolf Steiner, *Social Issues*, lect. of Mar. 18, 1920.

53 Ibid.

Notes

54 This passage, as well as the first paragraph of each of the following sections, is from Rudolf Steiner, *Guidance in Esoteric Training* (Forest Row, UK: Rudolf Steiner Press, 1998), pp. 24–27.

55 Rudolf Steiner, *Occult Science* (op. cit.), p. 311, tr. adapted.

56 Rudolf Steiner, *Social Issues*, lect. Jan. 5, 1920.

57 Rudolf Steiner, *Social Issues*, lect. Mar. 18, 1920.

58 Rudolf Şteiner, *Origin and Goal of the Human Being,* lect. Mar. 30, 1905.

59 Rudolf Steiner, *The Search for the New Isis: Divine Sophia* (Spring Valley, NY: Mercury Press, 1994), CW 202, lect. Dec. 26, 1920; also *Universal Spirituality and Human Physicality: Bridging the Divide* (Forest Row, UK: Rudolf Steiner Press, 2014).

60 Rudolf Steiner, *Knowledge of the Higher Worlds and Its Attainment*, p. 220, trans. adapted.

61 Rudolf Steiner, *The Festivals and Their Meaning* (Forest Row, UK: Rudolf Steiner Press, 1996), tr. D. S. Osmond, lect. of Dec. 24, 1905.

62 Rudolf Steiner, *Social Issues*, lect. Mar. 18, 1920, p. 124.

63 Johann Wolfgang von Goethe, in: *Goethe's Fairy Tale of the Green Snake and the Beautiful Lily* (Blauvelt, NY: Rudolf Steiner Publications, 1979), pp. 35–36.

64 Albert Einstein, in Ronald W. Clark, *Einstein: The Life and Times* (New York: Avon, 1972), p. 37.

65 Rudolf Steiner, *Where and How Does One Find the Spirit?* CW 57, lect. Jan. 14, 1909; tr. T. O'Keefe from *Wo und wie findet wan den Geist?* (Dornach, 1984), p. 210.

66 See, for example, Rudolf Steiner, *Knowledge of the Higher Worlds and Its Attainment* (op. cit.).

67 Rudolf Steiner, *Social Issues*, Jan. 7, 1920, p. 79, tr. adapted.

68 Rudolf Steiner, *Man and the World of the Stars* (Anthroposophic Press, 1963), CW 219, lect. Dec. 31, 1922, tr. adapted.

69 Ladinsky (ed.), *Love Poems from God*, p. 23.

70 Rudolf Steiner, *Awakening to Community*, lect. Mar. 3, 1923.

71 St. John of the Cross, *Dark Night of the Soul*, tr. E. Allison Peers (Image, 1959), tr. adapted.

72 Rudolf Steiner, *The Threshold of the Spiritual World* (Forest Row, UK: Rudolf Steiner Press, 1975), CW 17, ch. 9, p. 135, tr. adapted.

73 This is a rewording of a thought by Rumi; see note 10.

74 Rudolf Steiner, *The Threshold of the Spiritual World*, chap. 9, p. 136.

75 Rudolf Steiner, *Occult Science: An Outline* (Forest Row, UK: Rudolf Steiner Press, 2011), p. 357, tr. adapted.

76 Rudolf Steiner, *Macrocosm and Microcosm* (op. cit.), lect. Mar. 31, 1910.

77 The quoted words are from a participant who later wrote his recollection of the given Imagination. This version from Rudolf Steiner, *The Foundations of Human Experience*, tr. R. F. Lathe and N. P. Whittaker (Hudson, NY: Anthroposophic Press, 1998), CW 293, lect. Aug. 21, 1919, pp. 47–48.

78 Rudolf Steiner, "Rendering of Society: The Fundamental Social Law," CW 34; in *Understanding the Human Being* (Bristol, UK: Rudolf Steiner Press, 1993).

About the Author

LISA ROMERO is the author of several books on inner development, a complementary health practitioner, and an adult educator who has been offering healthcare and education enriched by Anthroposophy since 1993. From 2006, the primary focus of her work has been on teaching inner development and anthroposophic meditation.

Her first book on inner work is *The Inner Work Path: A Foundation for Meditative Practice in the Light of Anthroposophy* (2014). This was followed by three others: *Developing the Self through the Inner Work Path in the Light of Anthroposophy* (2015); *Living Inner Development: The Necessity of True Inner Development in the Light of Anthroposophy* (2016); and *Sex Education and the Spirit: Understanding Our Communal Responsibility for the Healthy Development of Gender and Sexuality within Society* (2017).

Through the Inner Work Path, Lisa offers lectures, courses, and retreats for personal and professional development, in communities and schools worldwide. These are offered throughout the year in communities worldwide. Lisa's capacity to deliver esoteric wisdom with insight and understanding allows her to meet the diverse needs of communities and professions.

For many years, Lisa lectured on health and nutrition and male/female studies at Sydney Rudolf Steiner College, where she continues to give lectures on inner development to the tutors.

Since 1999, she has been presenting on the subject of gender, sexuality, and spiritual life. She has been working with Waldorf schools as a part of their "health and wellbeing" curriculum, working directly with the students, teachers, and parents on this theme. Lisa has contributed to and is an adviser for the "Health and Personal Development for the Australian Steiner Curriculum Framework." She has developed training courses and facilitates professional development on this subject for teachers and health professionals.

Lisa designed and facilitated EduCareDo "Towards Health and Healing," which has offered eight-year courses focused on working with therapists from all modalities, as well as with Waldorf teachers toward cultivating the depth of anthroposophic insight through practical applications of therapeutic and pedagogical methods.

Lisa Romero is a contributor, tutor, and director of Inner Work Path, EduCareDo, Developing the Self – Developing the World, and the Y Project. EduCareDo is an organization facilitating long-distance self-awakening study in the foundations of Anthroposophy. Developing the Self – Developing the World offers community education, and the Y Project supports the transition of young people into healthy community life.

For meditation courses and talks,
see InnerWorkPath.com

For more information on school and
community Education, see DevelopingTheSelf.org

For online course material for the
foundations of Anthroposophy, see EduCareDo.org